BREAKTHROUGH SUCCESS

with MOETINI TIHONI

ALSO FEATURING
OTHER TOP AUTHORS

© 2021 Success Publishing

Success Publishing, LLC
P.O. Box 703536
Dallas, Texas 75370 USA

questions@mattmorris.com

All rights reserved. No part of this book may be reproduced, stored in a retrieval system, or transmitted in any form or by any means - electronic or mechanical, photocopy, recording, or any other - except for brief quotations in printed reviews, without the prior permission of the publisher. Although the author(s) and publisher have made every effort to ensure the accuracy and completeness of information contained in this book, we assume no responsibility for errors, inaccuracies, omissions, or any inconsistency herein.

Table of Contents

1. Success As A Choice 1
   by Moetini Tihoni

2. How To Deal With An Unsupportive Spouse In Business 7
   By Matt Morris

3. The Person You Could Have Been 13
   By Steve Moreland

4. The Magic Of Time 21
   By Arjan Scholten

5. Going Against The Grain 27
   By Ben Dahl

6. The One Secret To Long Lasting Fitness 33
   By Bernard Yeo

7. Never Ending Journey 39
   By Carolyn V. Anderson

8. Face Your Grizzly Bear 45
   By Chris McIntosh

9. Overcomer 53
   By Cindy Cavazos

10. Self-Image And My Identity 63
    By Devon Kurz

11. Milk And Honey 71
    By Dominika Blum

12.	The Magic Of Living Outside Your Comfort Zone	79
	By Helen Kithinji	
13.	I Choose Me	87
	By Ilioara Ormenisan	
14.	Seven Living Generations	93
	By Ilze Strauta	
15.	Achieve What You Want	101
	By Iréne Wrigstedt	
16.	Reach	109
	By Joan Kenyon-Woods	
17.	Unleash Your Power Within	115
	By Josef Buchmayr	
18.	The Power Of Faith	121
	By Leslie Freeman-Wright	
19.	How Moms Can Change Lives And Improve The World	127
	By Maria Helena Paulo	
20.	The Key For Limitless Success	135
	By Mike Howren	
21.	Living The Dream	141
	By Richard Denning	
22.	The Ultimate Success Formula	147
	By Romacio Fulcher	
23.	Shades Of Grey	153
	By Samantha Jung-Fielding	

"Meeting Moetini has been one of the greatest encounters of my life. He is someone with great social intelligence, a rare quality to find in today's society. He has never been able to conform to any laid down system, and that makes him unique, free in thought and word, an autodidact following his heart and his own beliefs. Since I've known him, I've never seen him cast down by failure. On the contrary, he has overcome failures with a snap of his fingers, which is why I consider him a real role model to follow, plus he is always trustworthy. I am so proud to have him in my life and to be his niece, and I am looking forward to seeing him evolve as an author."

—Ms. Otime T. Bavoil
Chief Operating Officer, Polynesia Consulting

"We've known each other for a long time: Moetini used to be a co-worker, and he quickly became one of my best friends. I know that I can count on him, no matter where he is around the world. Personal butler, receptionist, manager, whatever the field in which he works, he has always excelled. I have never had any worries for him; he is so talented and so confident in himself that it will take him beyond even his own dreams. His belief in himself makes him at ease with everything he undertakes. I look forward to seeing his next projects—he's exemplary! He knows how to make the right choices, for him, his friends, and his family. His self-motivation and personal determination give me such a boost. I am convinced that he can inspire anyone who crosses his path. I want him to be proud of me, as I am so proud of him."

—Mr. Anthony Eonet
French Gastronomic Chef for Billionaires

"Moetini and I have known each other since the early 2000s, and we've been besties ever since. Back then, I was far from imagining all the adventures that we were going to have together. I recall that when he returned from his studies in France, his head was full of smart ideas and his mentality had evolved in such a huge way. He has developed an extraordinary autonomy, independence, and thirst for discovery that allows him to succeed in everything he wants to, and thus overcome his fears. In all his diverse experiences, he has always made sure I benefit, and, thanks to him, I have also discovered countries and cultures, something I will always be grateful to him for. When he decided to leave for Bora Bora to work in the luxury hotel industry's challenging environment and thus develop meaningful skills and experiences, I thought how much he had always impressed me with his audacious mindset. He's traveled around the world alone and is afraid of nothing, always ready to start over and bounce back in adversity. He is constantly positive; even in the worst situations, he always bounces back, adapts, analyses, and rushes in to put things right. He does not regard responsibility as a burden but as an asset. As a leader, he possesses an inner force that drives him to make decisions that no one else on our islands can make because of fear of failure. Failure does not frighten Moetini; I don't think the concept even exists in his reality. He will succeed whenever, wherever, and in whatever he decides to achieve."

—Ms. Tevahinemoea Chaves
Chief Accountant Gras Savoye, Willis Tower, Watson, Tahiti, Member & Treasurer of TED-X Papeete

"I met Moetini four years ago through his fiancé, who is my best friend. I immediately recognized his powerful leadership capabilities. But today, I tell myself that what I saw in him then was nothing compared to what I see and know about him now! He is dedicated and persistent, with a mindset of steel. He is the friend and leader that we can count on and with whom we want to move forward. Capable of doing anything necessary to lead his crew, like a ship's captain ready to brave all dangers and protect his sailors, I am grateful to have this person on my life path. Not everyone is born with leadership skills, but with Moetini, it is innate, and that is why he does what he does and arrives where he is needed. The Will has wings. No one can stop its flight; this Will is called Mr. TIHONI MOETINI."

—Mrs. Francesca Todeschini
Director, WorldVentures | Inspirational Speaker & Mentor

"I've welcomed my little brother with open arms and consider him as such, even though we do not have the same father. I've watched him growing over the years and seen a strong and courageous personality develop, always knowing when, how, and what to do. He has a temper, of course, which I would say has caused us some differences in the form of sibling quarrels. Despite everything, he has always been very respectful. I like to say that I have been educating him on that path. I am so grateful to have him in my life and am one hundred percent sure he feels the same. He's always known how to face life's difficulties; his perception of the world is different from ours, which is a tremendous quality and has opened doors to many opportunities that he has managed like a master. This mastery and expertise will take him even further. I know that family has a meaningful importance for Moetini and that we can always count on his generous soul if needed."

—Mrs. Judith Manava Tauira
Head of Department Australes Navigation Company & Sister

"From dream to reality, Moetini (meaning 'Little Dreamer' in Tahitian) has learned to make his little dreams into big realities. Indeed, he just knew how to get lost and go in all directions to find himself fully and create a meaningful life. His professional and personal journey may seem chaotic to some, touching on so many things, as he experienced the pleasures along life's winding path. However, it was in being surrounded by darkness that he found his most beautiful light—in himself. Today, I see that he is a brilliant executive, working sympathetically with his teams. To conclude, Moetini is a person who can significantly change your life, and hanging out with him is a real blessing."

—Mr. Henry Terou
Businessman, Owner & CEO of Polynesia Consulting & Hospitality Industry Expert

24. The Immaculate Journey Of A Faithful Warrior. 159
    By Serah W. Muiruri

25. Rescue Mission 167
    By Sheen Marshall

26. What Most People Don't Understand About Network Marketing. . . 173
    By Steinar Pettersen

27. From Go To Woe . . . And Back Again 181
    By Stephen Davis

28. Just Decide - There Is No Other Option 189
    By Steve Eastin

29. Perception Is Everything 195
    By Syen Yap

30. Pulling Your Own Weight 201
    By Toni Catchings

31. Choose Mentors And Appreciate Failures. 207
    By Tonika Bruce

32. Dreams Are For Suckers 215
    By Whitney Tello

CHAPTER 1

SUCCESS AS A CHOICE

by Moetini Tihoni

I recall all the years I've struggled with personal identity. I'm a native Polynesian pure-blood (huh!) with a bit of French, German, Chinese, and British blood thrown in. All these different cultures have forged my personality, with the most prominent being Polynesian. I'm an island-dude with multi-cultural aspirations, but I've always seen myself as a human living on Planet Earth more than someone with an immobile, categorized ethnicity.

Ever since I was a kid, I've always been a rebel, even though my surroundings forced me to toe the line and stick at doing things *their* way, be influenced by *their* thoughts and *their* lives, because that's how it should be. The educational system is quite simple in our islands. Even though we have a strong French academic school structure, the anchored Polynesian culture goes beyond that, dealing with emotions (actually not *dealing* with them), so it's pretty confusing and challenging to sort out. Well, at least, that's what I thought. The reality isn't as pretty as we make it out to be. Deep in our souls, we all have a bubble our minds have created to protect us and keep us from collapsing. I buried, deep in my mind, these horrible memories of the abuse I suffered; although I can't tell I was forced, I did lose my innocence way too early. I grew up hating myself, my body, for a very long time, and all of a sudden, one fine day, I finally stopped moping about myself and made the choice to be happy. I deserved it. Our mind is an inexhaustible source of strength and energy. I had found the power to forgive that disgusting act and live with complete serenity. I've never shared it until now.

I am the son of two middle-class administrative worker parents, pretty much like every typical family (dare I say), with simple goals to achieve: work during your shift, finish at 3:30 pm, then back home to get dinner ready, enjoy your meal while watching the news and sharing your day at work/school and get used to making them proud of having at least average grades in most subjects. Apparently, that would lead you to be able to live a sufficient lifestyle: owning a car and a house, with loans at the bank that you'd have to pay off for the rest of your life, isn't that inspiring? Yay! I was limiting my brain by accepting the average. "You can do way better than you know, but it's still a great result," my mum used to tell me, and she turned out to be right. I always dreamed of being someone special and aspired to have an "amazing" life, like those of movie celebrities and famous singers. I've had my dreams broken so often that I'd prevented myself from dreaming big, discouraged by criticism and harsh realities. Most folks are just happy with an average, peaceful life on our little island paradise without much ambition for anything save for what's needed to live happily ever after.

I had no complaints. I've cherished my life with my parents, who offered me everything I needed. I also have a half-sister who is older than me. She was a maternal figure to me. I remembered my dad taking us to resorts on some weekends, events organized from his work. That's when I started to enjoy leisure time, tanning in the sun lounger, sipping virgin cocktails, while the adults busied themselves with their own activities. I was in love with the idea of being lazy, and I swore to myself that I'd live this way forever. Daddy got me back in the real world and simply goes with "Scratch for daddy with your lucky fingers!" meaning if you wanna be rich. I thought he had the dream job—traveling around the world. Travel. WOW! He was actually traveling to other islands for his work. He was away for six to 10 months a year. My strong mum took care of me by herself most of my life; we'd been facing difficulties together. I always admired her forthright and unconditional love even though I was not an angel, I must admit.

Growing up with the thought of living a cozy future—"Daddy's job is pretty comfortable, think about it"—just wasn't for me, as rebellious as I was. When I came back from France, with a few marketing skills and an excellent knowledge of wine (not to mention night-clubs and parties), I decided to reroute to the hotel industry, perhaps unconsciously. Indeed, tourism is my country's main economic activity. I knew I'd be dealing with foreigners, Americans, and maybe I would be able to get close to the lifestyle I always wanted; who knew what opportunities would open up for me? I loved that idea, but if I had to put that feeling into words, I'd say that I didn't want to work for them. I actually wanted to be like them. Dreams, again! That was the unconfessed desire, deep inside my heart, that made me want to change my life into something I never really dared to think, or rather dream about.

I didn't have any other way off the islands except through success in my hotel industry career and setting my sights on a management position. So, I chose to move to New Caledonia for a resort opening, which would lead me out of my country for good, and perhaps a long-awaited better lifestyle. I actually found love there. I'm so proud of her because she has always stood by my side through thick and thin. Before leaving that beautiful "Kanaky Rock," I was shown what could have been—the opportunity of my life whose call I dared to refuse. Was I not ready? Did I mistrust network marketing? Who knows? I was sure that I couldn't bear seeing myself in hotels anymore; I had enough of that thankless job. Well, maybe I hadn't chosen the best year to quit my career.

It was a pretty challenging time for both of us (my mom included). My girlfriend and I were hit by a car while riding a scooter on our way to job interviews. That accident left Aurélia badly hurt and unable to walk without a walking-stick for months. We were broke, unemployed, and back living in my parents' house. My pride was hurt. I felt so ashamed of myself, but, of course, I tried my best never to let it show because my friend—Ego—thought of it as a weakness. Then, my dad had a stroke, a bad one, that had paralyzed him ever since. Watching that proud man being taken down so easily by those teeny tiny little blood clots—my dad, whom I'd been fighting almost my entire life to avoid resembling him, an uncontrollable violent man as soon as he drank, whom I learned to tame, often by force, to protect myself and my mum—was utterly knocked out by the stroke. It felt as if I was meant to come back home during that time. It seemed that maybe our guardian angel had driven us back home for that reason. As we say, life goes on, and what I recalled repeatedly in my mind was that my mum had retired for over 20 years and still struggled with money. My dad had only just retired. That made me feel bad for both of them. I couldn't help but wonder at the time if that was going to be my future as well: working until my 60s, only to end up sick and enjoying retirement in a medical facility with money issues.

But then, amid all that struggle, I had an excellent job interview and landed a sales job for one of the most luxurious Polynesian brands, selling our famous Tahitian cultured pearls. After a short time, I was promoted to head of the Bora Bora site, so we had to move back to paradise after having first settled everything for my parents. I couldn't help feeling doomed.

Back in Bora Bora, again! With our famous Tahitian style sarcasm! - "*Hoki faahau I Pora Pora!*"

While handling my job to the best of my abilities, I wanted to develop myself by learning new business skills. I thought I'd learn as much as I could about entrepreneurship. I got some good ideas for initial projects and even finalized business plans. I started the reprogramming process, thinking differently about my life and about the things that I might really be capable of. At that point, I had only taken a glimpse of my true potential just by making the right choice for myself and my family. When we knew we had our baby girl on the way, my mind went into overdrive with even crazier plans. What would we do to welcome her?

I'd respectfully chosen to ask my father-in-law his permission to propose to his daughter. Then I had planned a trip to Vegas to ask her to marry me with a personalized diamond ring. We found out about the pregnancy the day after I proposed at the top of Sky Tower. Thank goodness! Otherwise, my story would have been different! I believe that these kinds of events that happen in our lives are not accidental. Law of attraction—that's the secret. I'm sure of it because Aurélia and I had openly expressed our wish to the universe to become a family, to be married (at least, I always wanted it secretly, but, again, didn't show my "weakness" or true self). Okay, so I wasn't going to be a celebrity after all, nor a famous artist in music or cinema.

As you may have picked up by now, my dream had always been to be wealthy-healthy, to travel all around the world visiting its the wonders, old and new, eat all the cuisines offered, and enjoy all the different cultures, while sharing it all with the people I loved the most. My closest friends and family will testify that I have always been a good person. Although it has to be said that I don't always keep my mouth shut, untold truths have slipped out. But, hand on heart, I have always welcomed people to my table, my house, and enjoyed company with whom I would share an excellent dinner and a few bottles of good wine.

Since the economic crisis caused by COVID-19 that hit us in 2020, I noticed that I started to become who I always criticized: the average man, always blaming life, bosses, the government, the school system, people in general, my parents, and my fiancé for anything I found faulty. I started to realize this even more when I began to listen to personal development podcasts, videos, and the training events I attended (thanks to the company that I'd finally chosen to enroll in). I was extremely grateful for having made that choice, the opportunity for a life change, and all I had to do was say YES. Well, my fiancé made me choose, to be honest. When they say 'listen to your women', just do it. So, who or what should we blame when life seems to make us average?

Previously, I'd always look at my life streaming by, without any purpose or any sense of having control over it. I thought I'd always be the dumb funny guy who loves to amuse his friends with jokes and stories, just an average man who is merely happy avoiding the stress of hard work, who will never overcome his untold fears, who drank until he forgot having a life purpose, and partied with no high expectations for himself at all. Did I truly have no other choice? I did! I've had enough of blaming others; I was done. I've proven it by becoming a better version of myself, the professional expert I am now, the super fiancé I am now, and, finally, the best soon-to-be dad I was going to be.

My beautiful little baby girl, Miss Lagresle-Tihoni Oranui Kyara UnaUnari'I, who was born on Saturday, July 4th, 2020, was the reason why I strived to be a better man—even the best version of myself thus far. Finally, I was unsure whether I had made a choice because I didn't really have the choice. That's how it should be. I have to be better because she deserves the best in everything—education, health care, lifestyle, vacations, etc. I want her to become an even better version of what we are now so she can play her part in enhancing the future of our world. I pledge and vow my life to be as inspirational, as committed to righteousness, as honest, as excellent a father and husband, and as helpful to other people as I can be in order to live positively and make our world a better place.

Changing our vision and perspective of life is simply a matter of being willing to convert a negative situation into a positive outcome. Have I mentioned that 2020 is a beautiful year? Let's continue to dream big—bigger than what we think our minds are capable of—by making the right choices for ourselves and our loved ones.

BIOGRAPHY

With a decade of expertise in the tourism and leisure industry, the "Maohi" Pacific Islander Moetini Tihoni made the choice of rerouting his career from regular employment to independent entrepreneurship in network marketing to help people achieve their life goals. He operates his organization in various countries around the world, especially in his home islands and current location, Bora Bora. While he has always been an authentic, high-standing, and professional person, he continuously tries to lift his colleagues and partners to the top in order to help them reach their true potential through trustworthy leadership. He shares with vulnerability and an open heart; that led him to a new path because he stands for truth and will always be true to himself. Today, he feels much gratitude for being a happily engaged man and a father.

Moetini Tihoni's contact details are available at https://linktr.ee/moetini

CHAPTER 2

HOW TO DEAL WITH AN UNSUPPORTIVE SPOUSE IN BUSINESS

By Matt Morris

In the process of leading hundreds of thousands of entrepreneurs and salespeople over my twenty-five-year career, I've witnessed that relationship turmoil is one of the single biggest killers to success in business.

Nothing saps your energy or drains your spirit more than disharmony in the household.

Before we dive in, I want to make it clear . . . I'm no relationship Goo-Roo.

I'm divorced, so taking relationship advice from me might be a bit like learning how to get six-pack abs from a sumo wrestler.

So, while I'm no relationship expert, I am an expert in human nature. I've coached thousands of entrepreneurs over my career, and relationship disharmony that impacts negatively on business development is one situation that I've been able to coach many others through successfully.

Many of you reading this may not have this issue or may not even be in a relationship, but you must read this anyway, because, on your journey to leadership, this WILL undoubtedly be an issue for some of the people you lead.

My training here is assuming you're in a committed relationship, either married or headed in that direction.

7 WAYS TO OVERCOME AN UNSUPPORTIVE SPOUSE IN BUSINESS:

#1 Don't push

Are you pressuring and pushing your spouse to be as excited about your business as you are?

I know your first instinct is to say, "No, of course not."

But, if I were to ask your spouse if they're feeling pressured, what would they say?

If you suspect there is even a slight hint of this, I'd recommend you ask them and get their perspective on things. If you want them to understand your dreams and desires in business, then I suggest you follow the sage wisdom of Dr. Stephen Covey: *"Seek first to understand, then to be understood."*

The more you push, the more likely it is that you'll create conflict. Some people aren't wired for entrepreneurship or, at least, don't believe they are because of their beliefs. Instead of pressuring them to be excited, you should be you and let them be them.

If you want your spouse to support your dreams and desires, you first must try to understand their dreams and desires and make sure you support them, even though it might be difficult at times to fully understand each other's goals.

#2 If you want support, give support

How exactly are you giving support in the ways that your spouse wants the most?

Notice, I said, "in the ways that your spouse wants."

You may be providing money, a home, doing the cooking, and cleaning. Those may be important for you, but, in many cases, spouses aren't supportive because they don't feel supported in the ways that matter most to them.

How can you BE the example for support that you want to be? The answer may not be obvious to you, so you may need to dig in, ask, and work on resolving that question until you find the answer.

To sum it up, you must be the example.

#3 Neutralize the threat

In many cases, an unsupportive spouse is unsupportive because they feel as though your business is a threat to the relationship. They may feel that you consider your business a bigger priority than the relationship and that your business is pulling you away from them.

You need to understand that this threat may not be vocalized because your spouse doesn't want to appear insecure or controlling. However, the reason they are not supportive could be because of their underlying fear and insecurity about the relationship.

For many entrepreneurs, this is hard to understand: in your mind, you're "doing the business for them" or for the family, and you've told them that. However, you must realize that even though that might be true for you, and even though you've told them that time and time again, they aren't feeling it.

So, how do you get them to feel it? Keep reading . . .

#4 Honor them

Find ways to admire and acknowledge what you honor and respect about your spouse.

Whether we want to admit it or not, we all have a desire to be respected. If your spouse feels as though you're respecting your business or your business partners more than them, it will drive a wedge between the two of you.

If you want to be supported and honored as an entrepreneur, support and honor your spouse and other family members from whom you want support.

#5 Appreciate them.

On a daily, yes, DAILY basis, take steps to ensure that your spouse feels genuinely appreciated. Of course, it's great to tell them, but folks generally see better than they hear, so make it a regular practice to write little letters or notes of appreciation for them. Even if it's just a sticky note, it shows that you care and make them feel appreciated and loved.

When you're out working on your business, take a few minutes to send them a text message appreciating and acknowledging them. I've seen relationships transform through the simple act of an appreciative text or sticky note sent every single day.

If you feel as though you've tried everything, then try writing a text or a note to send them every single day for the next thirty days and see what happens.

Reward the behaviors you want.

When your spouse shows any sign of support, go overboard in showing your appreciation for that support.

#6 Unconditional love

In our heart of hearts, what we all want is unconditional love—to be loved no matter what.

When your spouse is unsupportive, understand that it's likely because of their fears, their lack of feeling supported themselves, their lack of feeling honored, appreciated, or loved. So, show your love for them, no matter what.

If you want them to support you, whether you're winning or not, love them whether they're demonstrating love for you or not.

Act to ensure that your spouse understands that they are the most important thing in your life and show that you love them, no matter what.

#7 SUCCEED

I've seen hundreds of people go from unsupportive to being their spouses' biggest fans when they see their spouses winning.

There's an old story from Tom "Big Al" Schreiter that fits here . . .

A husband gets involved in network marketing. He's super-excited and has a dream of buying a new Cadillac. He cuts out a picture of a Cadillac and tapes it to their bathroom mirror. But when he gets home that night from work and a busy day of doing meetings, his unsupportive wife takes the picture down and puts it in the drawer.

But, undeterred, the husband tapes it back up on the mirror. Then, when he comes home the next night, again, it's in the drawer.

This process repeats every day for months.

Until one day, the husband comes home with a brand-new Cadillac, bought with money earned from the profits of his new business.

The next day, when the husband comes home, taped to their bathroom mirror is a picture of a mink coat!

Your spouse wants to see you win, but they might not believe it's possible.

So, do all the things necessary to win.

BIOGRAPHY

Author of the international bestseller, *The Unemployed Millionaire*, Matt Morris began his career as a serial entrepreneur aged eighteen. Since then, he has generated over $1.5 billion through his sales organizations, with a total of over one million customers worldwide. As a self-made millionaire and one of the top internet and network marketing experts, he's been featured on international radio and television and spoken from platforms to audiences in over twenty-five countries around the world. And now, as the founder of Success Publishing, he co-authors with leading experts from every walk of life.

Contact Information
Website: http://www.MattMorris.com
Company website: http://successpublishing.com/

CHAPTER 3

THE PERSON YOU COULD HAVE BEEN

By Steve Moreland

If Fate's blood-stained cauldron has not found your life yet, she's hiding just over the horizon, waiting until you're at your most vulnerable. So if you're willing to listen to someone that knows about life's ash heap, I'll share the Lessons I learned after I failed my Test. The lessons focus on our thinking. More specifically, about how thinking differently empowered me to thrive where most cannot imagine surviving. I promise not to waste your time with fluffy bullshit or rah-rah! Just the mental tools what worked, that brought me across a desert wilderness of 5,544 days.

May the following battle-tested advice return you from your seemingly impossible cauldron *"tested—and found not wanting."*

We Texans pride ourselves on our Code. Toughness is Rule #1. And it means *"no tears allowed."* See, our cult-like indoctrination begins the moment we are born. And the other Spartan rules include: *do only BIG things*, especially if others say it can't be done; *rub some dirt on it* because blood and scars prove your worth; and *do Right*, even if the Lord God, himself, threatens you to do otherwise!

Brutal. Absolutely! But definitely the kind of folks you'd want covering your back in a fight. It's a belief carved deep in our soul—that there simply is NO FREE LUNCH. It is a creed rooted in commitment and perseverance, summed up in one word. Grit!

The standard we have to carry begins early. At age twelve, I started *"earning my worth."* My phone rang off the wall with grass-cutting jobs in the Texas infernos called summer because my dad drilled me to do what everyone else is afraid of, to deliver results beyond expectations. Just self-disciplined results! No excuses.

I went right to corporate America after graduating with academic scholarships – working for three Fortune 500 companies before I was 24. At twenty-five I was in charge of my own brokerage firm in Dallas. By thirty, I'd made it to millionaire status, flew in private jets, brokered 9-figure deals from European castles, banked in numbered Swiss accounts, and spoke on international stages raising millions for venture capital deals.

Ballistic was my term for the vertical climb I experienced. Simultaneously serving as vice president of offshore operations for a boutique hedge fund, CEO of a 58-office tax and wealth management firm, and co-principal of a SaaS startup. I couldn't afford the luxury of sleep. And part of every month, I lived near my office in the banking district of Nassau, Bahamas, acting as the vice president of business development for a middle eastern banking syndicate.

Occasionally, I woke up at a place my then-wife and children called home. It was there that I slowed down enough to rub some of that Texas dirt on my hand tremors from sleeping only on those overseas flights. I was stumbling forward just to maintain the pace.

There was something wrong but I could not risk failing the mission. My Dad's standing orders were crystal: *"You can rest when you're dead!"* And this belief came from his creed that a man only earns a medal on his gravestone if he dies "in combat."

Well, I failed to become a "lifer" in the Corps, so I determined that I was going to achieve whatever most would call impossible. I believed in his invincibility! And after eighteen years of his Marine-style bootcamp, I feared only one thing, **"meeting the person I could have been!"**

So, when Fate's blood-stained hurricane came for me, I was Ready. Ready to blindly march into Hell itself. But after the first few years, I felt more like the Greek myth of Sisyphus who was sentenced to pushing a boulder up the mountain every damn day and then waking up the next morning to find it at the bottom again. I remember thinking to myself, "Maybe God is *not* good" after feeling soul-crushing agony for the first time. Real pain that made me wish I could just die and get it over.

I'll admit, all that invincibility crap did NOT work. And I'm painfully embarrassed to admit that I found myself wallowing in my self-pity after losing absolutely everything and feeling abandonment by all I loved. I had succumbed to that state of a *victim*. And you know what, that Texas dirt did NOT fix the wounds I'd caused my family for the undeserved trials and tribulations my bull-headed foolishness caused.

Though I was brought up with my dad's relentless Texan and Marine Corp code of conduct mixed with my mom's Christian beliefs, the devasting pain caused me to question their beliefs. Sitting in the ash heap of my life like the Bible's character Job, I commenced to blaming God for not protecting us from the horror that imprisoned us. I begged and even prayed for an instant release of misery, even raising my fist in anger and shouting "You're *NOT* a good god!"

I just wanted that magical snap of a finger and everything to be like it used to be. But genie-like fixes never happen, do they. Why? Because strength is *not* forged in luxury and comfort. Medals do not get pinned to your chest for holding hands and singing "Kum Ba Yah."

The struggle to endure real agony, to eat suffering, and know your pain so intimately that you name her has a purpose. You see, it took time for me to get over my self-entitlement in order to face my demons and do the most excruciating thing I'd ever done. Realizing that I could not change the past or erase what my mistakes had cost my family, I had to make a decision: either continue to blame others and wallow in self-pity or use the hell I was inside to forge a better version of me!

In school, we're first taught the lesson that prepares us for the test. But, in life, we face the Test first; later, we learn the Lesson.

The grade is what we become through it all. It's pass or fail. And yes, hell is when you meet that person you could have been. It means rising again and again within the blood-stained cauldron of Fate. Only this repeated discipline distinguishes the few from the many, the extraordinary from the ordinary. The worthy from the worthless.

But that person you could have been is only Hell if he or she stands better than you chose to become! **Hell, then, is meeting the *better* person you could have been.**

Like I promised in the beginning, what follows WILL take you through any hell. And you will arrive on the other side, *"tested – and found not wanting."*

Let's begin with a question: "Have you ever been really curious about something—to the point of obsession?"

Since I was a kid, I wanted to unravel this thing called thinking. I reasoned to myself that if I could only understand how the few we call "great" actually thought, I might be able to be like them and make the world a little bit better. Because, for the most part, they are human just like me. The only difference is that they *see things differently* in their minds.

Personal development "coaches" blather about managing our thinking. It is THE key, agreed. But it's not enough to know *what* to do. We've got to know *how* to do it. It's the subtle and often <u>hidden difference between learning science without the art of knowing how it applies to real-world situations</u>. Most of these "well-meaning" coaches deserve an "A" for science but an "F" in art. Never earning a medal from within Fate's blood-stained cauldron means their theories can get you to one destination – that chance to meet the person you could have been.

Here's an example of a coach with earned rank, Dr. Viktor Frankl – author of *Man's Search For Meaning*. Frankl didn't just survive six years of Nazi concentration camps, he changed the world forever with his discovery of how we create meaning through our imagination.

Better thinking creates better doing. And better doing creates a better being.

Frankl forced me to think. I mean really think. And all of a sudden, what Professor Eli Goldratt wrote in *The Goal* became crystal clear. "If we continue to do what we have done, which is what everybody else is doing, we will continue to get the same *unsatisfactory* result." But I asked myself, isn't that what we do so very often - more of what everyone else has done and then expecting a different outcome?

We are what we've done, right? So, aren't our own actions - what we *do* - that creates who we *become*? In short, "doing creates being." So, who we are today – our being, is a product of our past doings? Becoming someone better can only happen by doing differently. And differently results from the seed of the thoughts in our imagination.

Because I wanted a different future – one that honored the sacred by making the world better, I could no longer afford to think like I used to, or like everyone else. Maybe you're brighter than me and already know this. But for me, this realization was the Eureka! And in that realization, I felt something deep inside like lightning.

If my prior thinking caused my current doings (my actions and habits that are known as my reality), **then why couldn't I change my future by changing the way I was thinking?**

Socrates (Greek philosopher 470 B.C.) taught a Secret passed through his student Plato to his student Aristotle (Greek philosopher 384 B.C.). Aristotle planted this Secret into the mind of a 13-year-old prince. This Secret method of thinking changed the ancient world.

At 16 years of age, the prince led his cavalry at the Battle of Chaeronea, decimating a supposedly unbeatable enemy. At 20 years of age, he became king of Greece, marched his army towards Persia, solved the riddle of the Gordian Knot, and destroyed any that opposed.

At 24, he captured the supposedly unconquerable city of Tyre. At 25, he became Pharaoh of Egypt and then returned to the desert near modern-day

Babylon to lead his 50,000-man army against a force exceeding 500,000 led by the Persian emperor Darius. Charging into the front line on his legendary black stallion Bucephalus, he achieved the impossible and became emperor of the known world.

By age 30, he had created the largest empire in history. Today, he's still studied in war colleges for his battlefield genius, ethical governance, and unrivaled valor.

The Secret thought? "Be as you wish to seem."

The Result? One *impossible* difficulty after another - CRUSHED!

His Name? Alexander

How is he remembered? Alexander—the Great!

In school, we're first taught the lesson that prepares us for the test. But, in life, we face the Test first; later, we learn the Lesson.

Here's my experience. The Lessons learned *after* the Test lead to better actions—which lead to becoming a better being, right? That means that tests uncover our weaknesses so that we can learn greater lessons. What and who we become through the Tests reflects our grade in life.

If we're honest, we'll admit that we often create our own storms. And then we blame others when we must endure them. But if we use the agony, we find something called grit. Grit is commitment bathed in love to become better than we were the day before. It's a relentless dedication to rise—to become better, stronger, and wiser. It's a refusal to quit, even when we feel we can't get up again.

The question is, will we? Will we persist after the problems that were caused by our poor thinking – and the results that followed? Or will we just quit due to the fear of failing and the probability that life won't be easy?

Being *"tested and found not wanting"* means we'll certainly be scarred from one battle after another. But the scars reflect rank, defining how many times we returned to the cauldron instead of hiding and waiting to be rescued by the God that's testing us.

It may be cliché, but our very thinking sparks our every action. Put another way, our doings, added together over time, construct our being - *what* and *who* we become.

Do we dishonor the Sacred, settling for what everybody else is doing and continuing to get their same *unsatisfactory* results?

Or do we ***think* better**, in order to ***do* better**, so that we could ***be* better**?

We become what we choose to be. This is the Secret. My gift to you, as Aristotle long ago shared with Alexander, "be[come] as you wish to seem."

Now you know that Hell is NOT meeting the person you could have been.

Hell is meeting the *better* person you could have been.

BIOGRAPHY

A native Texan, Steve Moreland is known for two things. Dedicated practice. And success. Success equates to one's level of practice. So he really does only one thing. His Rubicon system teaches how to perform the common under uncommon conditions.

Motivated by the Latin creed FORTES FORTUNA ADIUVAT – "Fortune favors the brave," his mission is to deliberately cause affirmative outcomes that would not have occurred otherwise.

Connect with Steve via LinkTree: https://linktr.ee/steve_moreland

CHAPTER 4

THE MAGIC OF TIME

By Arjan Scholten

Time is life's great enigma. What is more mysterious than time? But what exactly is it, and what does it mean to us, as humans? And, perhaps most importantly, how does it work? In the course of my life, I've spent a lot of time thinking about time—and I believe that many of us are driven from time to time to ponder about the puzzle that time, as we know it, presents to us. And now, I'd like to invite you to spend a little time with me.

I was born in the Netherlands, and, as a young boy, suffered from a disease called asthma. It was challenging for a child to live with the disease. Although, in time, the disease would prove to be both a burden and a blessing in my life. When I was in my first year at primary school, I spent more time either at home or in the hospital because of the asthma. That was also the year that my parents got divorced. Because of the illness, I was made to repeat that first year of school, to make up for the time I had lost. You can imagine how I felt; it was a tough time, and it was difficult to connect with my classmates. I remember thinking that doing the same year over again at school meant that I would lose a year of my life. It's generally true that when you're young, you want to grow up fast. You want to go to bed late and do all the things that grown-ups are doing. Time never seems to go fast enough for you. Or at least, that's how it feels.

Over the next few years, my asthma became a real issue. I was 10, and my parents decided that it really needed to be dealt with. So, they started to search for a healthier environment for me to live in, hoping that things would improve and I would learn to live with my asthma. They came up with two options: One was an asthma center based in Switzerland, the second was another clinic located in the Netherlands. That's how I ended up staying for 15 months in the clinic in the Netherlands, far away from my parents, family, friends, or anyone familiar. I felt lost and often wondered how the time spent in the clinic would benefit me. But, at the same time, I began to realize that maybe I should look at the experience differently. Like it or not, the one thing that never changes for all of us, human beings, is the fact that you live by yourself and, therefore, experience life by yourself. This was an incredible insight for me. At that young age, I learned that I alone was responsible for connecting with people, forming my opinions, and living my life in a way that made sense to me. Some people might call this a kind of freedom. It was undoubtedly true that the idea of the constraints of time took on a completely different meaning for me than previously. I realized that there is no such thing as a time constraint because it's only a matter of what you believe. How you spend your time and what you do during the time you spend in this world is entirely up to you. Based on my experience, my advice is to spend it wisely, for time is not coming back.

And so that is what I tried to do. I became the master of my own plan, not an organized plan, but one that unfolded based on life experiences. I finished attending MAVO secondary school in the Netherlands at the age of 17, and wondered: What do I do now? Again, time became an issue for me. It was expected that, like most kids, I would find a course of study, go to college, and eventually get a master's degree in some field. But was that really what I wanted for myself? I mean, what did I know of life? It goes by so fast and, besides, I had questions about what kind of life choices I should make. It seemed crazy to be expected to make choices about the right educational path to take. I thought that it might be a good idea for me to take some time to find out who I was as a person.

But could I actually do that? My mind was full of what-ifs. You probably know that feeling when your emotions seem to take over, and your good judgment becomes clouded. I felt so strongly that I needed more time to get to know me. So, I decided to leave my comfort zone and seek adventure! I still think it's really important to find out who you are and how you tick, and only then make the big decisions that will affect the rest of your life. So, at 17, I decided that, since life was happening all around me, I should do what I believed was going to be good for me!

I chose to find myself, to get familiar with the real Arjan and find out what he's about, before making any of those big choices. Up to that point, my life had been dictated by my upbringing, my disease, and a somewhat limited view of the world. But my thoughts eventually led me to take a great leap forward into the unknown and embark on a big adventure: I decided to go abroad and live for a year in the United States, where I would attend high school. That would give me a chance to see how well I could manage and learn more about myself. It was a scary thought but, at the same time, full of promise and with the potential to be very rewarding. You could say that I took a whole year out to study myself, Arjan Scholten. What a great decision that was! By taking that time out, I learned so much about life and myself. I'd say that it saved me years of struggling to find my purpose in life, and gave me time to shape my own beliefs and goals that I could stand by. My life plan began to emerge—or, at least, I felt that I had an idea that, if acted upon, could become a life plan.

At last, it seemed that my mission in life was clear. Best of all was the realization that I had the whole of my life to make it happen. What a gift, and what a time saver! Unlike many other people, who go through life, not knowing what to do, when they're older, are left saying: "God, I wish I'd done so-and-so, but now I'm too old, and there's no time left to live my dreams." Not for me!

After spending a year in the US, I returned to the Netherlands, a reborn young man of 18. During my time away, I'd discovered that I had skills and decided that I would use education to help me master them. I went to college and eventually earned myself a bachelor's degree in commerce.

I started working and became a CRM expert—that's Customer Relations Management. I believe that everything in life, whether it's to do with business or your personal life, is about the dialogue we have with one another. We, humans, communicate with each other all the time. That's how we relate to people—by giving time to each other. Back then, I felt strong and worked hard on the goals I'd set for myself, but, unfortunately, I forgot my health and the fact that I have asthma. I was working hard and playing hard and generally enjoying life. But, while doing that, I forgot that my system, my body, needed proper care and that my life-work balance needed to be in sync. I needed to establish healthier eating habits and exercise more often. Things came to a standstill when I was 32 and was hospitalized with severe lung problems. Before I knew it, I found myself in intensive care, multiple tubes going in and out of my body, and fighting to survive.

The doctor told me, when I came in, the condition of my lungs was like that of an 80-year-old. In other words, like those of someone who had not taken their health seriously at all.

I am very fortunate to be alive today. After spending three weeks in the hospital, I was finally released and able to go home. But, what a time I had at the hospital! When I was conscious and transferred from the intensive care unit to normal medical care, I had a lot of time to think. I lay awake for hours in bed, my life flashing before my eyes, as I realized that this might be it—my life could be over. I could have died right there and then: A young man who died at 32 due to a severe asthma attack. What a way to go! That was also the moment that I finally understood the wisdom of "health before wealth."

That was a hard lesson for me to learn and comprehend. It took me another six months of being at home to come to my senses. My pride became anger, then fear, and finally gratitude, gratitude for life, for just simply being around and, hopefully, living happily ever after. So, once again, I made a life plan.

That plan contained everything. I'd learned from my experiences and the reason why I made the decision to enjoy life, to make the best of the time I have. Now, I make it my mission to inspire and help people by giving them—time:

- Time as a gift.
- Time to listen.
- Time to explain.
- Time to learn.
- Time to experience life.
- Time to feel.
- Time to express themselves.
- Time to love.

That's what I have learned: Time is magic. Scientifically speaking, you can say that a day has 24 hours, a week has 168 hours, and a year lasts for 365 days, which accounts for 8,768 hours. The United Nations estimate of the global average life expectancy in 2019 was 72.6 years; if we round it up—73 x 8,768—that equals 641 thousand hours. What do you mean, you don't have time? You have all the time in the world! But that isn't all: Our experience of time is governed by our perception of time. As we grow up, our view of the world and, thus, our perception of time changes. Isn't it a true blessing and gift that time is so amazing? And it can be spent in any way we choose. But just bear in mind that once spent, that time won't come back—so my advice is to spend it wisely.

We forget that time is just an instrument, and that our lives and our time occupy only a short period from a universal point of view. We humans feel, love, and experience all sorts of other emotions. And that is a good thing. That makes us special. So, be proud of yourself, and don't worry about the choices you've made or are going to make. Time is experience, so experience it. I believe that everyone has their own life journey and that the most important thing is to make it count.

Of course, people live and die, so why not make life a great journey? Take time to think about what you want your life to be about. How would you like to be remembered? What will be your legacy? Remember, your life is over before you know it. But, as long you're here, enjoy it and make the best of the time you've been given. I wish you all the best. May this chapter serve you as time well spent.

BIOGRAPHY

Arjan Scholten is a CRM expert whose passion is to help people and businesses, educating them about how processes can work in their favor. He's a big fan of personal development and learning how to have more fun in the workplace, and life in general. His mission is to inspire people and help them live life to their full potential. He believes that, no matter what your past, you can move forward and live your dream, simply by working passionately towards achieving it. Arjan's motto is: Live your life and make it happen.

Contact Information
Facebook: https://www.facebook.com/ArjanScholtenTime
Instagram: https://www.instagram.com/arjanscholten71/

CHAPTER 5

GOING AGAINST THE GRAIN

By Ben Dahl

I still remember looking at that number, thinking, "I can't afford this." The $2,000 was more than I had in my bank account, and it would be the first time I had spent that much on anything. There I was, pacing around my disheveled room in a run-down college house in my torn sweatpants. It was an environment best suited for living life between beer cans and bottles of dip spit, but I was somewhere else in my mind. I believed I could do something more, and I was about to make one of the biggest decisions of my life.

That is not to say that things were bad. I had a part-time job at a digital marketing agency in downtown Cincinnati. My boss had practically guaranteed me a position after graduation if I stuck around. I had earned membership in the most prestigious (and fun) fraternity on campus. I was dating an intelligent, kind, and beautiful girl. My social circle was so big I couldn't leave the house without seeing one of my friends. I rocked six-pack abs, held a position in the best business clubs on campus, maintained a 3.9 GPA in my honors program, competed in intramurals, and was hitting my stride in guitar practice.

Forgive me for sounding arrogant—life was good. You're probably thinking: "Dude, you had it made!" and I did, in a way. I had it made insofar as I could have easily gone with the flow and achieved a relatively standard, white-collar quality of life without having to try.

So, what on God's green earth could possibly lead me to take all of my money, including student loans, to buy a $2,000 online course on how to start a consulting business?

The simple answer is that "I wanted more."

Like so many of us, the path I was on at the time didn't reflect my dreams.

Do you ever feel that you were destined to do something great, something the world would recognize, something that would make a difference?

I think this feeling is familiar to you, to me, to the greeter at Walmart, and to the cashier at McDonald's. I believe that we all desire greatness and fulfillment in our cores of being, even if we don't know what that means for us yet.

It's a trope, but we all have our versions of success. I didn't know what mine was at the time, but I did know was that despite the positive momentum in my life, I couldn't settle for less than I was capable of achieving. I had heard tons of stories about kids my age and younger earning themselves hundreds of thousands of dollars from their businesses, and they had all of the freedom in the world to mold their lives to their liking—I wanted in.

So, I did it. I must have walked a mile in that little house before I pulled the trigger, but I did it—I bought the course.

Betting big on yourself is a strange feeling. It's somehow easier to bet on a football game, a horse, or even a poker hand. When you bet on yourself, it's do-or-die. Everything is in your control, and success or failure comes entirely by your own doing. There is an immense feeling of freedom mixed with a dose of "what have I done?" but whether you find yourself confident or afraid, there is only one course of action—to move forward.

I dove into the course, waking up early and staying up late to take notes and learn the material. The first item of action was to create a vision and a plan for execution. The following weekend, I skipped the big fraternity party and locked myself in the library for two and a half days to avoid distraction. I must have seemed like such a loser, but that was the weekend my world changed.

That weekend, I hardly checked my phone. I visualized my dream life and put it into a PDF that I printed and kept by my bedside. Once my dream life had been mapped out, I created a one-year plan to keep me on the right path, with detailed instructions on what to do each day for the next 365 days. In theory, all I had to do was follow my own instructions to get what I wanted.

My plans changed about two weeks later when my boss sent me to a business marketing meetup to hear an expert speak on new marketing strategies. After some tertiary research, I discovered that the speaker had spent one BILLION dollars in online ads. He was also running ads for the Golden State Warriors in their prime, and he had worked with dozens of other Fortune 500 companies. I prepped some questions, sat in the front, and took notes. That presentation shattered my paradigm of how the Internet worked.

After the presentation, I stuck around to say thank you and introduce myself. I shook the lecturer's hand with all of the eager energy I could muster and pitched my vision to him. It must have made an impression on him because he told me to apply for an internship, and I got the position.

I still remember the morning I went to work to tell my boss that I had to hit the road, effectively forfeiting my guaranteed job after college. It was tough, but I had to trust my gut and seize the opportunity.

Things accelerated from there. Within two weeks of meeting my mentor, I was flying around the country, engaging with some of the biggest names in marketing on the planet, and working on international brands.

I flew out to California for a marketing conference where I met the organizer. He assigned me the position of lead marketing specialist for a professional sports team and hired an international team under me. We were even featured as experts in training videos at GoDaddy's offices in Scottsdale. My mentor personally coached me, day in and day out, and I was learning faster than I ever had before.

The coming months tested me in every possible way. One night, while visiting family back home, my brother and I were walking the dogs around 10:00 p.m. when my phone rang. It was my mentor on the line. His plane had turned around on the way to a conference, and he needed me to fill in for him the next morning in New York City. I had never presented the material before, and my mentor was a 25-year industry veteran. How could I possibly fill his shoes? Nevertheless, I rushed home, booked my flight, practiced until 4:00 a.m., and woke up to catch my plane at 5:00 a.m. I made it to the conference to deliver the presentation with about an hour to spare.

One time, I worked two back-to-back, 95-hour weeks in front of the computer, not counting bathroom breaks. Moments like these pushed me to rise to the occasion. I had to learn on the fly with limited time and focus and roll with the punches. I also learned the power of a good mentor. For the first time, I saw the life lessons I had learned. These experiences must have shaved a good decade off my traditional learning curve—in business years, I would be pushing 40 soon.

I took a semester off school to focus on work, but in conspiring fashion, things came to a halt. I worked excessively, and my relationship floundered because of it. My mentor had taught me so much, but I couldn't keep up, and I stepped away. I did too little too late to save my relationship, my lease at the college house was up, and I moved home without a job, no girlfriend, and a semester behind in school. To save money, I also stepped back from my fraternity, which would cost me the friendships I'd spent so much time building. What had I *done*?

I tried to start a new business with some guys I had met on the road. To avoid the shame of returning to school as a failure, I took a semester of online classes from home at the same time. It wasn't long before the business ended in arguments, and I was forced to return to campus or lose another semester. Those were dark months, and my new college house seemed to reflect the state of my spirit. I moved in with roommates who left food rotting on the ground next to the trash can. Talk about high-class living! I stayed up late, distracted by TV shows, and I even picked up smoking to affirm my internal dismay.

It was in those months that my bank account went all the way down to $0 (actually less than that because I overdrew my debit card), and I had to ask my parents to cover my basic living expenses for a month. That hurt. It wasn't long before that I was networking and meeting some of the most successful people in my industry. How had I sunk so low?

There were moments when I wanted to throw in the towel, finish my degree, and "get back on track." I even wrote a modified vision document that stated I would "finish my degree no matter what." I stopped trusting myself.

I couldn't bring myself to get a job, however. I couldn't "unsee" the success I once had. I couldn't silence the burning question in my mind: "Why not me?" It turns out that a yearning spirit is not easily crushed. Instead of giving up, I picked myself up, started to network, and managed to secure some projects that helped pay my bills.

Then, I got a surprising message from my mentor, offering me a second chance. How could I say no?

I finished my semester at school and went back to work with my mentor. It was just as challenging as before, but I was prepared. We flew around the world and back, working on massive projects. On one trip, I expected to be in Vegas for a two-day conference but ended up staying away from home for two months. Now, *that* is rolling with the punches. I went coast-to-coast across the United States, overseas to Taiwan, and even as far as the Philippines. There were times I slept on airport floors between 18-hour, non-stop workdays, but it was fun. My mentor helped me to save several more years on my learning curve.

The time eventually came for me to leave the roost and go out on my own with my newly found confidence and stronger skillset.

It wasn't a direct path to true entrepreneurship, however. I worked temporarily with another marketing agency to get back on my feet, though my first few personal clients were so challenging that I almost threw in the towel again.

I thought that maybe if I got a job for some security, I could grow my business part-time until it was "safe" to go out on my own, so I applied for a job and got an interview right away. An hour later, I had talked my way through three levels of management to the director of marketing at a $275 million company. They offered me the job with an annual salary of $50,000 per year with benefits, a paid vacation, flexible hours, and a "great opportunity" to earn a whopping 5% yearly raise. Now, I'm no mathematician, but 5% of $50,000 is only a couple hundred bucks extra per month *before* tax. That was when I knew that I could never work for anyone else. I knew that, if I focused my efforts, I could earn a 5% raise every day working for myself.

That was the last straw. I'd officially given up everything I once had—my degree, my girlfriend, my fraternity, my college friends, and my career—but something interesting happens when you abandon one path for another. At each major juncture along the way, you learn something new about yourself. Each of these lessons helped me mold and clarify what I want out of life, and I got closer to my vision with each step.

I met another girl who is beautiful, intelligent, and kind. I realized that no one cared if I had a degree. I learned not to work for money, but to make money work for me. I have a better appreciation for the friends I've kept. I'm in a fortunate position in that I have the ability to select the projects on which I want to work and the people with whom I want to work.

It's easy to follow the crowd. It's easy to do "what you're supposed to." It's easy to dream about having a better life. It's hard to bet on yourself. It's hard to stick it out and do the work. It's hard to pick yourself back up and break free of the chains of fear and doubt.

I knew I would never realize my dreams if I followed a traditional path. It was only by going against the grain have I given myself the opportunities to turn my dreams into reality.

BIOGRAPHY

Ben Dahl is an author, speaker, and business coach who has helped Fortune 500 companies grow online. Having spent millions of dollars in marketing and leading international teams, Ben has the technical and leadership experience to produce massive results. With his expertise in marketing and operations, he helps businesses expand through building scalable systems, uniting teams, and generating demand. Ben has spoken on international stages, led full-day workshops, and worked alongside industry leaders around the world to educate entrepreneurs on cutting-edge strategies for business growth. Ben believes that by helping others win, he can elevate more people to live life on their own terms. When Ben is not working, he enjoys long walks in nature, reading, and a good board game.

Contact Information
Facebook: https://www.facebook.com/BenDahlMarketing/

CHAPTER 6

THE ONE SECRET TO LONG LASTING FITNESS

By Bernard Yeo

Stand at a busy intersection and observe the people passing by. What do you notice? A significant number of people are overweight. In today's world, the internet and social media provide information about health and fitness in an instant, yet the number of overweight people is increasing.

If you struggle with being overweight or lack motivation for exercise, I might be able to help.

Being in a comfort zone makes us feel safe and certain in routine activities and habits, so we may feel that stepping out of this zone could bring unexpected risk and stress. For instance, if you've never been the exercising kind, you'll need the motivation to get started and stay on course, right?

Most of us know someone who had the sudden motivation to lose weight, whether it was to impress a girl or get in shape for the summer or a planned holiday. But once the girl moves on to be with someone else or when the event is over, the motivation disappears, and the weight gain returns.

You see, these motivations are external influences. It's not necessarily a bad thing. It is effective for jumpstarting a fitness program. I used to think all it required was enough motivation to act and succeed in getting healthy and fit. I soon learned it also takes determination and willpower to stay motivated, which is why so many people give up after a while.

So, how do some people make keeping the weight off look so easy? How do they stay so motivated for so long? What is the differentiating factor?

There is another element more powerful than motivation. And it is not another kind of motivation. I often wondered why I could stay motivated long enough to be successful at certain things while some of my friends couldn't. Then, I came across research by Dr. Maxwell Maltz, a cosmetic surgeon. He noticed that after correcting imperfections on his patients' appearances, some still felt they were ugly, and this led to his discovery of self-image. In his book, Psycho-Cybernetics, he said, "A human being always acts and feels and performs in accordance with what he imagines to be true about himself and his environment." So, it wasn't what his patients saw when they looked in the mirror. It didn't matter because they considered themselves ugly.

Self-image determines the actions and decisions a person makes every day. For example, someone might have a goal to lose weight, but he continuously sabotages his efforts by overeating sugary foods. Why is that? His self-image is that of an overweight person and so his subconscious mind will consistently act in accordance with his self-image.

Effective weight management starts with motivation, but it won't sustain you. You need to program your subconscious mind and develop a good self-image to be successful in the long term.

Looking back on my life as an example, I started smoking in my early thirties. It probably started with friends over at my house. They wanted to smoke, and I wanted to be social. Soon I was taking smoke breaks with my work colleagues as well. But, after a few months, I didn't feel good about smoking. I felt that it wasn't me. Unbeknown to me at the time, it was probably Dr. Maltz's influence from the power of self-image. Perhaps my self-image of being a non-smoker came from my father. He smoked ever since I knew him and then he passed away from cancer when he was only fifty-one years old. Prior to discovering he had cancer, his engineering company still had hundreds of thousands of dollars owing to the banks for machinery leasing, loans, and recurring costs in operating a factory. My mother, my brothers, and I had to pick up from where he left off as it was our only source of income. It was terrifying because we didn't know anything about operating a business. Losing him was the hardest episode of my life and it was a shame that he couldn't teach us any business skills in time.

Not to brag, but I found it wasn't difficult for me to quit smoking as I had no withdrawal symptoms or nicotine cravings. So, despite the many people around me who smoke, I couldn't be influenced for long. While people normally fail to quit smoking, you can say that I *failed* in smoking!

Another significant event in my life was when I wanted to lose weight in December 2010. I was already in my late thirties and I had not exercised for years. While I was deciding on what to do, I found out that my cousin, Thomas, had just finished a full marathon. Ever since I was a teenager, I admired people who ran a full 42.196 km. I couldn't even run 5 km without stopping a few times. So, my cousin's success inspired me to get into running.

My idea of succeeding was to totally immerse myself in running. First, I set a goal to run a marathon in six months. Then, I bought a book on the beginner's guide to running a marathon. I started to train according to the plan in the book with almost no deviation. I watched proper running techniques on YouTube, I signed up for shorter races leading up to the big event, and I became aware of my food choices. I imagined myself running like Ancient Greek messengers delivering letters in times of war.

On marathon day, it was a tough and hot race. I had cramps in muscles I never knew existed. But I completed the race in five hours and one minute.

Over the next few years, I would run more marathons and even a 100 km ultramarathon. In 2018, I decided to shift from running to lifting weights.

In my marathon example, I was initially motivated to run a marathon in six months. I was motivated by my cousin's success. But, I also totally immersed myself in the sport, so much so that being a long-distance runner formed part of my self-image, which made me get out there to train, regardless if it was too hot or raining.

Now, we circle back to my original promise to you - to help you be successful in your fitness journey. I recommend you get started by motivating yourself and developing the self-image for long-lasting change. How long should you keep yourself motivated – until you achieved your goal and transformed your self-image.

Start your fitness journey with a reason. For me, it was my wife and children. I never want them to experience what I went through with my father's death. Write a letter to yourself (don't type on a computer) and tell yourself why you want to be fit. The letter can be any length, but the longer it is, the better. I want you to make a *promise* to yourself that you will achieve your goal. I say promise because breaking promises is more emotional than just missing a goal. I have taken out letters to myself written months ago and whenever I read them, I get emotionally charged.

Another powerful technique is to announce your goals on social media like Facebook. Letting all your friends know and holding yourself accountable can be incredibly powerful. You will get a lot of motivation and encouragement from your friends. Similarly, with your letter, on Facebook, you are promising your friends.

Build your self-image. Dr. Maltz said to change our self-image, we must use our imagination. By imagining a new healthier version of ourselves, our actions will be redirected to make it come true.

It can be hard to imagine because we are preoccupied with distracting thoughts, so meditation can be effective through implementing more of our senses to achieve our goals. So, here's what I want you to do: Take your self-image vision from the back of your mind and put it in front of your eyes by writing it out on paper. Again, there's something real about the act of writing things down. You employ the sense of sight, touch and hearing your written words in your mind. Create a vision of what you want to be. Put it on your desk or refrigerator and look at it everyday.

When You Don't Feel Motivated

Here's the other side to achieving your goals. There will be days where you don't feel motivated to do anything. You won't feel like going to the gym or for a run. I've faced laziness and procrastination too. There are some people who suggest dressing in a gym or running attire is motivating to get going. If you find an effective technique, then use it.

Here's what worked for me. When I was a runner, I told myself I'll only run for five minutes. If after 5 minutes I don't feel like running anymore, I'll stop. But, after five minutes if I feel like I want to continue, then I will run for another five minutes. Then I evaluate again if I want to continue or stop. I have run extra distances because of this mind hack. And, if your exercise is at the gym, tell yourself to go but only commit to do the warmup sets of your favorite muscle group, then decide if you want to continue the workout or not. You haven't failed if you stop after five minutes. Think of it as a sloppy day and let it go.

Another way to beat motivation (or lack thereof) is to integrate fitness into your life. Consider using resistance bands while watching television, set exercise time using calendar appointments, or have friends pick you up at scheduled times to go to the gym. Stick to these ideas and I promise you, you'll see the change in your self-image.

I want to close this chapter with the story about the scorpion and the frog. You may have heard of it, but I have a different view. The insert below is from Wikipedia:

A scorpion asks a frog to carry it across a river. The frog hesitates, afraid of being stung by the scorpion, but the scorpion argues that if it did that, they would both drown. The frog considers this argument sensible and agrees to transport the scorpion. The scorpion climbs onto the frog's back and the frog begins to swim, but midway across the river, the scorpion stings the frog, dooming them both. The dying frog asks the scorpion why it stung, to which the scorpion replies, "I couldn't help it. It's in my nature."

Just like it is the scorpion's nature to sting, you must establish a healthy self-image with fitness in your nature. If you do, you will never have to struggle with weight issues again.

BIOGRAPHY

Bernard Yeo is known for his love for personal development and dedication to personal fitness. Having run marathons for several years and switching to weight training, he has redirected his passion for coaching others on how to fight the battle of the bulge and gain fitness. With years of virtual traveling overseas and YouTube on his belt, he now makes actual adventurous and challenging trips with his ex-classmates every year. Bernard lives with his wife and two sons in Kuala Lumpur, Malaysia.

Contact Information
Facebook: https://www.facebook.com/BernardYeo
Instagram: https://www.instagram.com/justdoit.mindset/

CHAPTER 7

NEVER ENDING JOURNEY

By Carolyn V. Anderson

Success for me continues to be a never-ending journey of challenges followed by favorable outcomes. Pulling back the covers and getting out of my warm bed turned out to be the biggest challenge on this cold winter morning. I once worked for a successful attorney who told me that success started with waking up and getting out of bed every day with an attitude of gratitude. Years later, when I was going through the divorce process, remembering his words and enforcing that positive attitude saved me from falling into depression.

According to the dictionary sitting beside my computer, the word "success" has more than one meaning. Apart from gaining wealth and fame, it also describes success as achieving a favorable or desired result. The point is if you are happy with your outcome, you are successful.

For as long as I can remember, I liked sharing anything beautiful or unusual that I saw in the world around me. My father, an artist, taught me to sketch and reproduce my interpretation of the surroundings on paper.

I was immersed in sketching, doing it as often as I could find the time, thereby improving my skills. But the thought of making money from my art never occurred to me. In high school, an advertising agency collaborated with our school's art department and sponsored a poster contest with cash prizes.

The agency was in search of ideas for billboard advertisements for its clients. The design had to be simple but large enough for drivers and passengers in vehicles on the highway to see and read the message in a flash.

Our art teachers provided the poster boards and poster paint. I visualized my design and then sat down with paint colors to sketch and paint. When our posters were completed, the teachers submitted them to the agency's team for a decision.

On the day of the contest results, we all gathered in the school's auditorium. The first poster displayed on the stage was the poster for third prize. I recognized my poster and heard my name being called. I walked up to the stage with a bounce in my steps and a smile on my face to receive my envelope of cash.

As the second and the first prize winners received their envelopes, a sense of curiosity directed my attention to the other winning posters. I realized that even though I had submitted a well-thought-out and artistically-done poster, the subject of the other two winners was better aligned with the vision of the agency's clients.

First lesson learned—*always give the client what they are looking for.*

DEVELOPING SKILLS

I pursued my passion in college and majored in art and design. I also picked up new skills in architecture, blueprint layouts, and exterior and interior designs. In my oil painting class, our Instructor challenged us to use color to show line and movement on a new canvas. I had been up the previous night studying for an exam in my next class, so I chose to paint a subject similar to what I had studied. I created something different from my usual work. By doing so, I gave him exactly what he was looking for, and not surprisingly, that painting ended up in the university's gallery.

In one of my design classes, the Instructor gave us the taste of creating "light and dark" designs on photo paper. I was enchanted with the developing process in the darkroom. Seeing the images come to life in the developing trays reignited my passion for recreating beauty around me. It was a much quicker way to share images that would make others smile.

After college, as we stepped into the real world, only office desk jobs were available to women at that time. I was good at answering phones and could type, so a job downtown was not hard to find. I started looking for photography classes close to work as I did not want to put my new passion on hold.

I learned to be aware of the lighting and contrasting color shades while taking black and white photos. Acquiring new tricks of developing photographs, I experimented with my grandfather's 35-millimeter camera with a retractable "billow." I took photos during my lunch hours and sometimes after work.

Grateful that I had a salary and paychecks to rely on

Such was my passion that I started saving money to purchase equipment for developing photos. It wasn't long afterward that my closest friend and I made plans to fly to the New York World's Fair later that year. I was still living at home when my parents decided to move closer to my grandmother. As I wanted to move with them, I purchased an automobile to commute to work. In an effort to save money, my girlfriend and I drove to New York from Michigan in my new Chevy. With a newly-purchased Kodak Instamatic camera, which automatically advanced each frame after the shutter closed, our journey began.

I had enjoyed traveling to several states and Canada before college, so this was a much-anticipated trip. We drove straight to our hotel in New York. Parking my car in the hotel's garage, we relied on the subway system to get us to the fair and back. Everywhere we went, my camera accompanied me. I gained an appreciation for the quick shutter movement when we took the "ski lift" above the fairgrounds from one end to the other. I had a lot of photos developed by someone else and put together a photo album to show to family and friends who otherwise would never see the World's Fair.

Another detour before building a darkroom

I had finally saved enough money to purchase the necessary equipment for my darkroom. But by the time the equipment arrived, I had fallen in love and was planning my wedding. So, it went to storage at my parent's house.

I hadn't been to San Francisco since I was seventeen. My husband's friend lived there, so we flew to San Francisco for our honeymoon. I carried one of my cameras along on our tours in and outside the city and visited sights that I missed on my first time there. On the weekend, we flew down to Los Angeles to visit my sister-in-law's husband. She had come to our wedding, but her husband could not get off work to travel. It was the perfect opportunity to capture the city in its full spirit. The next week, we drove to San Diego—I had never been there and was eager to take photos by the water. A few days later, we were homeward bound flying out of the Los Angeles airport. Yet again, I sent the film out to be developed, but at the back of my mind, I was dreaming of my darkroom.

We rented an inexpensive apartment, which allowed us to save for a deposit on a home we eventually purchased. Our firstborn was five months old when we moved into our new home. There, I set up a darkroom and went to work in it, but it proved difficult. When our second child was born, it became almost impossible to make use of the darkroom. Remembering something I heard long ago, "Out of something negative comes something positive." I realized I still had my camera and knew where I could have my film developed. I was grateful to watch my children grow up and capture those precious moments on film.

When my children were in school, I opened up my darkroom. The photographs I developed were mostly shared as gifts; that would put a smile on the recipient's faces. The success I achieved could not be evaluated monetarily.

Several years later, in the process of divorce, I could no longer afford the cost involved in photography. I had a son and daughter in their mid-teens and a job that barely paid the bills. The photos and processing were not paying for themselves, so I had to shut it all down.

The thought of starting afresh and reopening my darkroom began to take shape when my children ventured out on their own. But without a plan, my enthusiasm for the process wavered. Out of the blue, one of my girlfriends asked me to share a booth with her at a local street fair. I created greeting cards to match her crafted door hangers—this plan ended up being mutually beneficial. So, we made plans to do it again the following year, and my daughter encouraged me to sell my photos this time.

As there were several craft booths selling photos, I decided to place my black and white photos on greeting cards. A friend of mine owned a printing shop with her husband, so I asked her for help. She showed me how to do the layouts, which they ran through the press on heavy stock paper. Then they scored the seam to be folded, and it was ready for the next step. I purchased envelopes for the cards and applied for a copyright. Grateful for her help, I suggested she keep a few cards to display as samples for their customers.

At the last moment, my booth partner backed out. With the help of friends and the women in the two booths around me, I set up my display. Pricing the "photocards" as single cards, I also sold them in packages of ten. I helped the two women next to me by watching their booths whenever they needed a break. They did the same for me. By the end of the two-day fair, the three of us had become friends. For the next four years, we requested the same spaces next to each other.

Battling the rainy clouds, the sun shone brightly on the day of the craft show. I was pleased with the successful sales of the cards. Michigan Lighthouse photoprints drew the most attention—coincidentally, they were my favorite. Now a new journey was materializing; to find other lighthouse enthusiasts and join them in visiting and photographing lighthouses.

I realized that success achieved through working with others is undoubtedly more fun. Finally, I had found an opportunity that made a positive difference in the lives of others. I discovered that as a team, we reached more people, identified their needs, and helped them find solutions. It was a whole new level of success beyond our expectations. When you only focus on personal success, you limit yourself. When each member of the team develops another person, and that person develops another who, in turn, develops the next, and the next, you will have a chain of people, a team, working toward a common goal.

I have often read that "You are the average of the five people you spend the most time with." Often visiting The Henry Ford Museum, old photos of three successful men come to mind—Thomas Edison, Henry Ford, and Harvey Firestone, who all shared a strong friendship. Surround yourself with the right people and build a network of successful people as your support group. The results may surprise you.

BIOGRAPHY

At a time in Carolyn's life, when most people retire, she is infused with a strong impulse to see what is around the next corner. She hopes that her story inspires you to pursue your dreams with passion despite the challenges life throws at you. She believes that "You only fail if you quit." She acquired her writing skills with the help of her high school journalism teacher. Carolyn recently joined other best-selling authors in *The Art and Science of Success, Volume 5,* with her chapter, "Finding Success Every Day." She learned teamwork and leadership skills through local and national organizations: parent-teachers association, 6-Area Coalition for Community Mental Health Board of Directors, and Parents Without Partners (as a program and education leader).

Contact Information
Facebook: https://www.facebook.com/CarolynsVerve

CHAPTER 8

FACE YOUR GRIZZLY BEAR

By Chris McIntosh

You are squatting on the bank of a snowy stream, filling your water bottle. As you watch the water flow into your bottle, a thought engulfs your mind—you will be forever lost in this unforsaken wilderness and die. You will never be rescued. Then, images of your family back home come flooding in. Your children need you to teach them about life. They are counting on you. And they have no idea where you are at this moment. Something kicks in, and you begin to strategize your way out of your situation, blaming yourself for getting into it in the first place. You hope to get rescued, for everything you have tried so far that didn't work. As your belly reminds you that it has been too long since your last meal, you rack your brain to find food and survive another night without freezing to death. You look down and see your tired reflection in the stream and think, "If I follow this, maybe it will show me a way out."

As your water bottle is almost full, you hear a noise in the bushes, upstream from where you are squatting. You turn, look up, and your eyes lock with a grizzly bear, who is now casually strolling toward you. The bear you thought you had escaped from days earlier, has found you again. Now, he is approaching you directly, and he is not coming to be your friend. Fear suddenly consumes you and dropping your bottle, *you run!*

We are all created with a purpose, destined to do great things in our lives. But why is it that most people lead what Henry David Thoreau called Lives of Quiet Desperation? For most people, the biggest regret at the end of their days is not the things they did and failed at, but those they were too afraid of doing. Not speaking up for themselves, not doing *that* thing they always wanted to do, not approaching the person who made their hearts flutter, or not making amends with a family member constitute some of those regrets. People regret being risk-averse and not starting that business they had always dreamed of; not taking enough vacations; not living the lives they were destined and created to live; of not having the courage to live lives they wanted instead of the lives others expected them to live; and of working hard all of their lives only to build someone else's business and someone else's dream.

Yet again, you have gotten away from the grizzly bear. But this time, you realize that it is only temporary—he will find you again. As long as you are in his world, he will sniff you out. You are no longer thinking about being rescued, about getting to a place of freedom. All you can think about is how this grizzly bear is going to take you out, and when it will happen.

As you're contemplating your demise, your thoughts revert to your future, to your family, to the things you still need to accomplish in this world, and at that moment, you make a decision—I must face this grizzly bear; I must kill this grizzly bear. How can you ever do that when all you have is a small pocket knife? Surely, a pocket knife could never penetrate deep enough into the bear's hide to do any lethal damage, but then you remember reading about how others had slain grizzly bears with nothing more than a spear.

We all have so much potential to achieve great things in our lives, but we've built these invisible and internal barriers. We are a powerhouse of so much information, skills learned through the books we have read, and from the life we have been living. Courses bought, money invested in the boot camps—yet we still do not have the success we deserve.

Why is it that success evades you? Is it because you didn't buy the right course, or you don't have the right information? Perhaps you didn't read the right book, or you just weren't born into the right family. The answer to all of these questions is "no." You have not yet arrived because there are grizzly bears in your life. Each time you begin to tread on the path of success, the grizzly bear is right there, waiting for you and ready to devour you. Ultimately, fear grips you, and *you run!*

One of the most popular acronyms for fear is "False Evidence Appearing Real." I have heard another one—"Forget Everything and Run." Fear is a powerful emotion and a primal instinct, which compels one to *run* in the face of danger. It consumes you, and if you let it control you, it ends up controlling your life. Eventually, you begin to justify the fear and consider it a new norm. "Living by default"—our whole lives, we are programmed to live a certain way. The problem with a default way of life is that it is just too easy. It is too easy to show up every day at the job you hate. But we justify it by saying, "At least, it's a paycheck." We are programmed to go to school and get good grades so that we can go to college and receive a degree (along with a mountain of student debt). And why do we need a degree? To get a job, of course, and they pay you just enough so you won't quit, and of course, you work just hard enough so you won't get fired. Besides, "they have great benefits," you say. I call this "the golden handcuffs."

Now, there's nothing wrong with getting a degree and having a job. But not having a plan to get out of that job when you want, is wrong. The greatest country in the world, the United States of America, is the most prosperous country in the world. People risk everything, including their own lives, to get there. Then why is it that even at the age of sixty-five, nine out of ten Americans will be living at or below the poverty line? Because living by default is easy. Even right now, as I write this, the economy is booming, yet many Americans will come up short when it comes to retirement income. The idea of being a greeter at a Walmart, when you should be enjoying your golden years, is not exactly enticing. According to the Pension Rights Center, half of all Americans at the age of sixty-five or older have incomes of less than $24,224 a year—far less than the amount most need to meet their day-to-day living and health care expenses. Yet, I am grateful for companies like Walmart that are willing to employ the elderly in our society who fall in the trap of a "default life."

"Face Everything And Rise"—my favorite acronym for fear. We all have grizzly bears or fear in our lives, but how we deal with that fear determines our future. The only way to design your life instead of living by default is to first slay the grizzly bear in your life. I am no different: I bought the books, the courses, invested in boot camps, but I never had any success. That is until I realized that my success had nothing to do with the information I had purchased. Merely hoarding information or knowledge wasn't enough; I had to take action. Most people's inability to take action reflects their deepest fears, current behaviors, current beliefs, and operating norms. Their assumptions and rigid patterns prevent them from living by design, and they resist any change in their lives. I once heard that the only person who likes change is a baby with a wet diaper. I was at a place in my life when I realized that I had grizzly bears preventing me from making change, and harvesting my true potential.

    I had humble beginnings, so I needed to overcome the invisible barriers to achieve success. As a young child, I often saw my mother rip pieces of paper called food stamps out of a book, as we didn't have enough money to buy groceries. The embarrassment of standing in line in that grocery store is still fresh in my mind. My father refused to go with my mother as he could not bear the humiliation. I don't have a college degree—my parents could hardly afford food, much less pay for college. I'm the oldest of six kids. My dad was in the timber industry—he was a logger, or as some people call it, a lumberjack. I love my mom and dad, and they did the very best they could with what they had. Unbeknownst to them, they lived a life of default. Our broken educational system fixates on how to score a job. To my parents, they did everything right—my dad was and still is a very hard worker. After the Vietnam War, my dad did the honorable thing that every father does. He went to get a job to provide for his growing family. He didn't have a college degree either, so he did exactly what his dad had done, and that was to go to work in the timber industry. And he taught me how to do the same—to be a hard worker—and that's what I did. I worked hard, and I thought that the harder I worked, the more ahead I would get. So, I followed after my father. My dad did give me some advice, though. He said, "Son, don't go into the Army and learn how to be a mercenary. Instead, go into the Air Force so you will at least learn a skill. So, you won't have to work in the woods your whole life."

    Following his advice, I went into the Air Force. Please, don't get me wrong—I am grateful for all branches of the military. It is because of our military that our country is as great as it is, and we have the freedom to choose to live by design. I would recommend my boys to serve in the military, as you can learn so much about yourself and discipline from the armed forces, but I also teach my children to live by design.

We all have defining moments in our lives. Reading this book could be your defining moment. I encountered mine during a conversation with a letter carrier. After getting out of the Air Force, I held various jobs, including working in the woods as a lumberjack. While working as a letter carrier at the post office, I met another letter carrier who had been working at that post office longer than I had been alive. At that point in time, I thought I had finally arrived. I had a government job—there was no way I could get fired, and the pay was really good. When I found out that this letter carrier had been delivering mail longer than I had been alive, I was blown away. I was in my early thirties, and the conversation had come to the place where I asked him how much money he made annually.

That question and his response was my defining moment. When he told me how much he earned, I realized that I could no longer work for the post office. At that time, I was earning more money than him on an annual basis. How could I be making more money, having only been at the post office for a short four years than someone who had been there for thirty-plus years? I blindly followed what my dad had taught me, and I worked hard.

> *"If you don't find a way to make money while you sleep, you will work until you die."*
> –Warren Buffett

I was trading time for money. I worked so hard that I requested to be on what was called the ODL, the Overtime Desired List. This concept may sound foreign to some: I worked ten to twelve hours a day, six days a week, and thus, I made more money on an annual basis than a thirty-year US postal worker who only worked a forty-hour week. But as is customary, my standard of living had adjusted to the money I was making, and I was not getting ahead financially. It hit me that I was not willing to work ten to twelve hours a day, six days a week for the rest of my life. I had a young daughter at home, Makayla, I adored her, and I wanted more children. I remember that I didn't have a lot of time with my dad because he worked so much, but I treasured what little time I had with him, which was usually only on the weekends. I cherish the time that we spent hunting, camping, and fishing together. I fondly recall that on weekends he would take me with him to the gym, and we would play a game of pickup basketball with all of his friends. I wanted to spend more time with my family and wanted that for my children, so I quit the post office to pursue a business that I hoped would get me to the land of financial freedom. Soon after, the grizzly bear came. Things got bad. I got divorced. Life turned upside down.

In the movie, *The Edge*, which I highly recommend you watch, Anthony Hopkins is being chased by a grizzly bear. He realizes that his only option is to kill the grizzly bear. It is the statement that he makes in the movie that changed my life, as I hope for this book to change yours.

He says, "What one man can do, so can another." I had long realized that I was destined for success in my life; so, all I needed to do was to learn what others have done to find success and then replicate it. I wanted to leave a legacy for generations to come, so investing in real estate made sense. For me, real estate investing was the vehicle through which I would create a passive income and free up my time. Over time, I learned what others had done to gain success, not just in real estate—because if it was easy, everyone would be doing it—but in life.

We all have grizzly bears that chase us down and prevent us from taking action, from getting to that place of ultimate success, and it is very scary. Your choice, whether you *Forget Everything And Run*, or *Face Everything And Rise*, makes all the difference. Remember, you do not have to carry the burden all by yourself: "What one man can do, so can another." Face your fears, slay your grizzly bears and change your life. Stop living by default and instead choose a life of design. If you won't do it for yourself, do it for your family, for your legacy. Is it scary? Yes! But you can do it. I believe in you.

BIOGRAPHY

Chris McIntosh has been an entrepreneur for over fifteen years. He has coached, mentored, and inspired hundreds of entrepreneurs and real estate investors over the last decade. He founded and is currently the president of the longest-running real estate investing club in his hometown of Spokane, Washington. He manages a multi-million-dollar real estate portfolio and helps others get into the game of business ownership and real estate investment. His mission is to inspire others and empower them with universal truths to lead a life of design. He is the proud father of Makayla, Austin, Noah, Caleb, and Jessica.

Contact Information
Facebook: https://www.facebook.com/mcintoc
Instagram: https://www.instagram.com/tip.real.estate/
Website: http://www.nextgenrei.com

CHAPTER 9

OVERCOMER

By Cindy Cavazos

I remember from a young age having to take care of my brother, who was a year younger than me, as well as a three-year-old child. At the time, it was just my brother, my mother and I; I didn't have a father in my life and knew nothing about him. The only other family I had was an aunt. My mom was single who often worked nights, so I was left alone to care for my brother and anyone else who was with us, and usually, instructions were left for me to warm or cook dinner. We must have been on food stamps because I remember the book of play money. We also moved around often, so I don't have any childhood friends.

One night, while my mom was at work, someone broke into our apartment. I was lifted from my bed and taken to another room. I woke up with a pillow over my face hearing whispers, while a cold metal object was pressed to my forehead. It was a gun. I couldn't see the man, but he was molesting me. When my mom came home, she found her gun had been taken with other valuables. I said I was okay after the incident, and it was never mentioned again. I was eight or nine years old at the time.

Later, when I had children, I did not leave them home alone until they were eighteen.

When I was nine, my mom met a Greek man, and they had a daughter, my sister, who I took care of since she was two weeks old. I remember staying up all night when she had colic. My mom was at work, and I had school the next morning. It was just our routine. My brother and I looked after our sister for many years while my mom worked. I recall sitting on the door frame of our 2-bedroom apartment in Houston with my siblings as the sun set because the light between our apartment door and neighbor's door was the only light we had. It wasn't a power outage. The light bill hadn't been paid. I think a neighbor called my mom to let her know our lights were out.

Throughout my life, my mom worked 2 to 3 jobs to make ends meet. She missed out on holidays, our birthdays, including her own, as well as Mother's Day. She also missed our school functions. During a school production of Hansel and Gretel where I played Gretel, I remember standing on the stage looking for my mom and nearly forgot my lines while looking for her in the ocean of faces. She wasn't there.

My brother and I were due to go on a field trip, and although I don't remember if it was through the church or school, I do remember asking my mom repeatedly to wake up and drive us there. We were late, and they were going to leave without us, but she couldn't wake up. When I came back into her room, she was trying to place her legs through a paper bag, thinking they were pants because she was still asleep. We eventually managed to wake her, and we made it to our field trip, but I will never get that image of my sleep-deprived mom out of my mind.

It was sometime in junior high when my mother met my second stepfather, who was all smiles at first. He worked and helped my mom with bills, and they too had a daughter, my youngest sister. He showed my siblings love, but he was addicted to drugs and alcohol. To this day, I don't know the substance he was taking. I just remember the syringes and glass pipes.

The abuse was subtle at first, which then started escalating from corporal punishment to verbal abuse to outright hitting me. It was during high school, either as a freshman or sophomore, when my relationship with God blossomed thanks to two young school friends. They invited me to a church where I started building a relationship with God who I adopted as my father since I didn't have one. On one occasion, my friends came to pick me up for church and my stepfather said, "The bitches are here for you." My stomach turned. How could he call the people who shed love and light into my life such foul names?

He had been drinking straight for days and had lost his job. One night he came into my room and hit me for no reason while sitting next to my sister. I called my mom and he denied hitting me. A screaming match followed and he threatened to kill us. He then left the house, and I told my mother I wasn't waiting for him to return to kill us, so I was leaving. She packed our clothes and we all left for a friend's house, where we stayed until my mom got a new apartment. After months had passed, my mom told me that my stepfather was coming back to be part of our family. I told her that if she chose him over us that I would leave when I turned eighteen; I was only sixteen at the time. She picked him.

We moved so much during my childhood that I couldn't tell you how many schools we attended. I asked my mom to let me go to the same high school for all four years, but she broke that promise when she decided to move our family to Florida for a business venture that summer. I left the few friends I had where I managed to be part of the drill team and played varsity soccer as a sophomore. Now, all of that was over and I had to start new. I tried to stay behind with my church family but my mom wouldn't allow it. I cried the whole drive to Florida.

Even though my stepfather had stopped drinking, he was still verbally abusive. I wasn't even allowed to have an open-air vent in my room; he would come into my room and close the vent. So one time, I removed the whole vent from the wall, and he ransacked my room looking for it. I started working as a cashier at the local grocery store and I needed to wash my work apron frequently because it got soiled easily with milk, raw meat, fruits, and vegetables. Yet, I was only allowed to use our washer and dryer once a week. Another time, I didn't wash the dishes properly at home and my mom came to my work to look for me. I hid from her and didn't go home that night. I stayed with aunt instead. Eventually I returned home.

I stayed busy, filling my time with school, work, and gym. There was a law school close by that I contemplated attending after graduating from high school. I asked my mom if I could, and she told me to ask my stepfather, the same man who bullied me daily. I knew then that I had no future in that household. I saved money to return to Houston and start my life there. I turned eighteen in the June before my senior year and told my mom I already purchased a bus ticket back to Houston and that she could not stop me from leaving. My stepfather and my mom sat me down, and he confessed and apologized in front of my mother, saying he had purposely made my life miserable. I believe this was my mom's attempt to get me to stay, but I knew where her loyalties were, and they weren't with me. I left my siblings and my mother, but I was ready to live a life without abuse.

That summer, I lived with a church family back in Houston, and circumstances made it difficult for me to enroll in school and finish my senior year. It was not easy to have my school records transferred as I needed the paperwork I didn't have. One day my church family said they were moving and no longer had room for me. I found my stuff in a bag at the church when I returned from a youth church retreat and found that my money had coincidentally run out too. I would contribute financially and do things like take the family out to eat and help pay for car repairs if they didn't have money, so I felt they used me until I was left penniless. I didn't have a car or a bike, so I had to depend on other people to give me rides. I asked a church friend if I could live with her; she was staying with her boyfriend's family. This arrangement didn't last long, so we both stayed with her mom who was living with another family. I didn't have any relatives in Houston, just church family. I moved from home to home and finally decided to go live with my grandmother in Monterrey, Mexico to try finish my senior year there. I applied to the local school, but they needed my school paperwork. I begged my mom to send it, and although she said she did, the papers never made it to the school. I worked as a teacher and a telephone operator to offset expenses and I took a bus everywhere I needed to go.

Meanwhile, my mother moved back to Houston. I wanted to finish my school so badly that I moved back to my mom in Houston, despite the fact that facing my stepfather would make me ill. With my stepfather's presence, it continued to be an awful living situation. I got a job in the same mall as my mom so we could share rides to and from work, but my stepfather said that I had to find my own ride. He would leave me there on the sidewalk, stranded at 10 pm, as he drove away with my mom. There was no public transport system anywhere near there, and I was forced to ask strangers for rides or call taxis. Day-to-day life was challenging.

My stepfather wanted me to start paying rent. One evening, there was an argument, I don't even remember what it was about, but I just packed a small bag and started walking. I had a high school friend pick me up and I lived with him. We became romantically involved but it ended after a phone call between him and another girl where he denied my existence, while I was living there. We fought and he threw me out. I didn't have anywhere to go; I was only eighteen.

I looked in the Yellow Pages and found the Covenant House in Houston where he dropped me off.

The shelter wanted me to take a GED course, but I refused and went to the local high school where the school counselor wrote a letter to the shelter stating they would allow me to finish my school year. The shelter let me continue living there while I went to school, but it wasn't easy. I had to share a room with three strangers. I had hundreds of dollars, clothing, and sentimental jewelry stolen from me. I walked into my room once to find a guy shooting up drugs. I worked, went to school, and lived in the shelter, which had very strict rules. Some of the residents could not adhere to the rules and were either kicked out or left of their own accord. Some of them, male and female, were consumed by the streets of Houston and turned to prostitution. I cried every night that I was there.

Another church family reached out and explained they were willing to cosign an apartment for me. After living in the shelter for three months, I was able to leave and lease my first apartment with the cosigner's help. I started working as a waitress nearby and managed to pay all my bills on my own. I was still going to school to finish out the year and graduate, but to do so, I had to take two buses from southwest Houston to the inner-city high school, which took over an hour. Then, a family friend gave me a '78 Chevrolet Monte Carlo to drive to school and work. It was an old car that was expensive to maintain, but it was still better than waiting for a bus in the rain. To finish my high school education, I had to take a night school class at MacArthur High School on the northeast side of town where there were regular drive-bys and high gang activity. I fitted right in with my '78 Monte Carlo and felt like I was in East Los Angeles.

I graduated from high school with an honors diploma. I didn't attend graduation because I didn't know anyone in the school and knew nobody who would come support me. After the first six months of living alone, I was able to transfer the lease for my apartment into my name solely. The boyfriend I lived with before the shelter, moved in with me and that was the beginning of a 20-year abusive and loveless relationship. I went from waitressing to working as a leasing agent in the office of the apartment complex where I lived. I took a year off from school to figure out what I wanted to study. The Monte Carlo engine died on me around the same time my stepfather did the same.

My mom called to tell me that my stepfather came home and was throwing up blood on the driveway. He was hospitalized and given a few days to live. My mom requested I go to see him, but I didn't want to; however, she urged me to go and I eventually relented. When I entered his room, he immediately sat up in bed, moving his arms and legs up and down uncoordinated. Obviously, he wanted to say something to me or even hit me one last time, but he couldn't utter one intelligible word. He died a few days later, and my siblings and mother were left alone once again.

I wanted to become an architect and decided to study electrical engineering at ITT. I worked nine to five and then attend school six to ten, Monday through to Friday. I was at the top of my class in college but in 1998, I became pregnant with twin daughters--one of the biggest blessings from God. I didn't think it was logical for me to pursue electrical engineering anymore because I was not going to put two babies in daycare. My daughters were born healthy. Their father and I decided I would continue to work because I made more money and had more benefits, and he would stay home with the twins. But, after about a month, I was ready to quit and be home with my daughters. We knew if we wanted to provide a future for our kids, we would either both have to work or move to Mexico where life was cheaper. Well, we saved, packed up and went to Mexico. I stayed home with the 2-year-old twins while their dad worked as a schoolteacher and gave private English lessons on the side. Yet, we still didn't have enough for food. I rented out our PlayStation in 30-minute intervals, then added snacks and drinks, but even then, the profit was just enough for us to eat. We sold our belongings at flea markets; we did what we could to put food on the table. God never let us go hungry. When we literally didn't have a dime to our name, a neighbor would come by and offer us a plate of food.

We had a very loyal customer who was ten years old, and I could always count on him to rent the PlayStation for 30 minutes every morning so that I could buy milk or eggs for the twins. It was interesting as this child was bullied because his mother would pick through everyone's trash to recycle paper, metal, plastic, and glass. He had nine siblings and his mother put the older children through college, and they were now lawyers and engineers. Even though he was bullied, he had more money in his pocket than any of the other kids, and they would often borrow from him as well as bully him. I favored this child. I treated him like my son and hated leaving him. My mom had put a bug in my ear about having another child soon, so I prayed that God would bless us with a son. I specifically asked for one boy, not two; otherwise I would have to sit on the floor of the car because we wouldn't have any more space for two extra car seats! Within three months, I was pregnant.

After the tragic event of 9/11, we returned home, and in the following month, our family was back in Houston. We were living with my husband's mother and brother, and that's when I began to realize where his loyalties lay. I tried to leave with my daughters, but his mother convinced me to stay. I shouldn't have. I should have walked away and never looked back. That's when I knew I had to make enough money to support myself and my children. I started the college enrollment process, but I didn't want to start until my son was a year old. My friends and family discouraged my return to school and discouraged me from becoming a nurse because of how hard it would be with three children.

I finished nursing school in May 2006 and graduated with honors. I worked hard as a nurse and encouraged the father of my children to go to school. He began his college education shortly afterward, but it took him six years to finish, during which time he did not work. After he graduated, he couldn't find a job. No one would hire him. I was so blinded, I made excuses, but ultimately, I didn't know any better. I didn't have a father other than God. I didn't have uncles or any good man in my life, just abusive stepfathers. I didn't see the red flags even though everyone who knew us did, and they tried to warn me. When he choked me for the first and last time, I moved out but I didn't file for divorce because I had done that before and lost a lot of money.

In 2015, I filed for child support, and when he found out how much he was going to pay, he contested custody in the Attorney General's office. To afford a lawyer, I started working more and more, but I was tired of working weekends and holidays. The hospital owned me. I spent more time at work than at home with my kids. I barely saw my kids. I remember at one point, I was on the edge of my bed crying on the phone to a friend about not wanting to go back to work. Then, one day in September, everything changed when a good friend called and showed me this amazing concept. I only had enough money in my bank account for rent that was due in ten days, but I knew that if I didn't do something different, then nothing would change. Knowing that God was placing something very important in my lap, I took a leap of faith, and this concept has been a blessing in our lives ever since.

In June 2016, my ex took my son and refused to return him. When I went to pick my son up, we both called the police. He told the police I assaulted him, but I never put my hands on him. On the contrary, he was the abuser. The police believed him and arrested me, but they couldn't charge me with assault because I never touched him, so they charged me with burglary of my own home. There I was, handcuffed in front of the house I built for my family and my twins in the Honda minivan I bought with my nursing salary. Yet, I had plenty of opportunities to have this man arrested, this man who lied to the officers and had me in handcuffs. Not only was my freedom in jeopardy but so was my nursing license. The same man I put through college for six years was taking away my freedom, my livelihood, and my children all on a lie.

I was treated like an animal in jail and wasn't allowed to use the bathroom for over five hours. I was later transferred to a maximum security prison where women were kept in glass cages. One of them asked me why I was there, and like in the movies, as I answered what my charge was, she finished my sentence. When I asked her how she knew, she said it was because she was in for the same allegation. I found out from her that she had been in for eighteen months, but if convicted, a person could serve two to twenty years. My knees buckled and my heart stopped. I could not believe what I heard. I did absolutely nothing wrong. I prayed harder than I ever prayed before and cried like I had never cried before. But God had a plan. That night, he gave me a vision that I would be reunited with my three children, and I saw us on a beach with blue waters and white sand, laughing and having fun.

I held onto this vision through nearly three years of court dates. I paid $900 to get out of jail, and thirty days after my arrest, my lawyer called and said the District Attorney rejected the case. Although I didn't have to go to court nor report to the board of nursing, the false arrest would still negatively affect me. My ex used this false arrest against me, which ultimately cost me more than my nursing license. The judge took almost all my parental rights away over my son. I was devastated and hurt beyond belief. I had felt no greater pain in my life. I paid five lawyers in total and also had to pay child support for my son even though I was taking care of our twin daughters. I worked almost every day in 2017 and only took off Thanksgiving and Christmas.

In June 2018, my mom called to ask me to move my holiday Tupperware out of her storage. I asked her jokingly if she was moving someone else in, and she said she was foreclosing on her 20-year home. She hadn't been working as she was taking care of my 99-year-old grandmother, whose caregiver of fifteen years had recently quit. I was crushed that my mother was losing her house. I couldn't believe I lost my home to my ex, and my mom lost her home to foreclosure. I swore I would never let anything like this happen again. In September 2018, I moved my mom and my grandmother in with us.

In early January, my friend Johnny called to invite me to a national training event that greatly impacted my life. I started building my business again. I ranked up and started earning residual income, as were my partners. I traveled more in those last six months than I did my whole life. I requested a meeting with my son and the judge accepted because my son wanted to spend more time with me, but my ex denied him that right. The judge finally interviewed my son and I've been granted additional visiting time ever since. I'm glad I never gave up when my friends and family told me I was wasting time and money on trying to get more time with my son.

My mom is one of the greatest women I know. One thing she taught me is that you can do anything you want to do. There is nothing that can stop you. God has given us the choice of right or wrong, and faith or doubt. Without God, without faith, I could never conquer the obstacles. I would have never survived my trauma. Ask, Believe, Receive, and Expect it. If I hadn't gone through the trauma I went through, wouldn't have a story to help others conquer their own obstacles! On many occasions, the following verse has reminded me of my path.

> "But they that wait upon the LORD shall renew their strength; they shall mount up with wings as eagles; they shall run, and not be weary; they shall walk, and not faint," —Isaiah 40:31 King James Version (KJV).

BIOGRAPHY

Cindy Cavazos has been a Registered Nurse for more than fourteen years in Houston, Texas. She obtained a national Critical Cardiovascular certification and is the single mother of three children, her 20-year old twin daughters, and a 17-year-old son. She homeschooled them all their lives, and now the twins are in their second year of college. One twin has a 3.4 GPA and the other twin has a 4.0 GPA. Cindy makes over $100k annually. She sacrificed family time and was unable to help family and friends achieve greatness because of her nursing job. In the last four years, Cindy built a small Network Marketing Business that now has a presence in over three countries, and the business growth is allowing her to spend more time with family and friends. She wants to help a billion people and change the world with this concept.

Contact Information
Facebook: https://www.facebook.com/cindy.cavazos.35
Instagram: https://www.instagram.com/p/B1k2SBKBEAK

CHAPTER 10

SELF-IMAGE AND MY IDENTITY

By Devon Kurz

Self-awareness is knowing where I am in life, how I feel about it, what I am doing, and where I am headed. Who I think and believe I am is not as important. It is detrimental to my growth and the impact of presence to believe in who I am not. I must change the way I see myself and have an understanding of my true identity—who I am, the purpose for which I was created as uncertainty breeds anxiety. This involves understanding who I am, who created me, and what I believe in. Do I believe what the world tells me I am, or do I believe it is my creator? I have struggled with this for the majority of my life…until now. I came to an understanding, a belief, after many years of fighting, pushing my body to its limits, working my life away, and thinking that I would get what I wanted as long as I worked hard and long. So, I took twenty-plus years, accomplishing many things except for the things most important in life: family, friends, marriage, and perhaps what is most precious, my beautiful children (Sierra and Conner), who are now young adults. I lost so many precious years and missed out on crucial developments in their lives as they grew up. I didn't see myself as the loving and caring father I wanted to be for my kids. I saw myself as the father who worked, providing money and not time. My identity was that of a workaholic and not the loving father I desired to be. After all that had transpired, I lacked any healthy relationships, I was in poor physical condition and health, and I finally came to realize that my life had to be different. I needed to change, though I didn't have the answer as to how to go about it. I didn't have a good mentor in my life—if I did, I wasn't listening, and I never realized it.

One day, a good friend and business acquaintance of mine invited me to look at something. Dustin said, "Do you have ten minutes to watch this video?" In all honesty, I didn't think I could afford to take the time given all the work I had to get done, but I said, "Sure."

I tell you what—it got my attention and gave me hope. I hadn't felt that excited for many years before and maybe ever. I thought that this was the answer for which I had been looking, and I would finally be able to get my life under control. I would have time to spend with those I love and go places with my kids, family, and friends. I believed that I would do the things I had wanted to do for many years.

I was going to be a millionaire—that was what I had told my dad and a man (who had come to sell insurance) when I was about sixteen years old. They were asking me questions for insurance purposes, and I said, "I don't need insurance—I'm going to be a millionaire by the time I turn twenty-five." They both looked at me and chuckled as if to say, "Yeah, right. That's not going to happen."

My heart sank, and my hope vanished for twenty-plus years because I chose to believe them. They had not done it themselves, nor did they know anyone else who had done it. When I saw the video Dustin had shared with me, my heart, my hope, shot up like a rocket! I felt alive again. I was going to do this. I was going to change my life. It felt like I had started a new chapter in my life's journey to fulfill my purpose.

I began to invest in myself more every day, using it as an opportunity to build a business that would provide for my family and friends. I was excited to help others achieve what they had hoped to accomplish for years but couldn't find that for which they looked. I knew I had something that would have an impact on thousands of lives and their communities to make a difference in the world. I decided that I would no longer work twelve to sixteen hours a day and seven days a week including holidays. I was going to travel and enjoy life. I invested some time into a business a few hours a week. I was making progress, had made a few ranks, had received some recognition, and I got back more than I had initially invested. It was a good start. I had never done it before, but I had a team to help me and the support of people who got no direct compensation for helping me. It was unbelievable! I will be honest: it felt good. I was energized by the ability to make a difference in my family's lives and futures. I was able to fit the business into my schedule and add another stream of income without taking away from my construction business. I thought it was great and simple—I could build the business just like I had Decor-N-More—the name of my construction business—by word of mouth. I had the right idea—at least, I thought I did, but it wasn't as easy as I thought it would be. I had started my construction business on a foundation of honesty, integrity, a strong work ethic, outstanding quality, and extreme cleanliness, and it grew by word of mouth. I became very well known for those values and fairly successful in the eyes of others. I believed I could give a repeat performance in the network marketing/direct selling industry.

When I started, it appeared that I would do just that, until I attempted to share my incredible opportunity with two of my best friends, who wouldn't even look at it. I know it wasn't their fault, as I hadn't brought it to them in the proper way. In other words, I didn't follow the system! My heart sank, and my excitement depleted. I wanted it more for them than I wanted it for myself. I felt sick and rejected. I didn't understand why, and I wasn't sure if I wanted to move forward with the business. What was going on? What happened? I no longer had the self-confidence I had with my construction business.

About a year later, a coach of mine, Scott Haug, introduced me to a program called "Thinking into Results" by Bob Proctor and Sandy Gallagher. Scott and his program, "Thinking into Results 2.0," which he had created in conjunction with "Thinking into Results," was instrumental in helping me discover the paradigm shifts in my life. I discovered the answers to many questions, some of which I had yet to ask. My identity is composed of my impressions of who I think I am, but more importantly, who I think I am not. You see, when my friends decided to not look into the business opportunity with which I had presented them, I had taken it to heart, as if they had rejected me, and my self-image went back to when I was sixteen and was laughed at because I would never be a millionaire. I had defined my identity as being a confident construction businessman. I felt secure in who I was and what I was doing. I had learned from and worked with my friend/brother, who was very knowledgeable and experienced.

Aaron (a.k.a. Harv) and I had worked together for many years. He had mentored and trained me to be knowledgeable in the field of construction, and the business was known for being reliable and dependable, even though I was not known in the direct selling industry, nor was I trusted to be experienced or knowledgeable. I did not identify with the industry as I had in the field of construction. So, when I had had a few more no's, and I was not able to handle the emotional impact of the rejection, I shut down.

My hope, my belief in who I was not, was reflected in my self-image and self-confidence was gone. I began to self-destruct and felt more miserable than I can describe. Many areas in my life started to fall apart, though I still studied the program and continued down the path of personal growth and development. I still listened to and attended coaching calls with Scott, but I did not know what I should ask to turn things back to moving in a forward direction. I also stayed connected with my business via leadership calls and events. I began taking a "Discipleship Training Institute" class through the Grace Community Fellowship—the Church I attended—led by my friend and pastor, Steve. You could honestly say that I genuinely was digging deep, and I was involved. My self-awareness was growing, and I began to take notice of what seemed to be seeking my attention—my self-image and how I pictured myself—as Bob Proctor would say, "Who I am not."

I don't consider myself religious, even though I was raised under the Church's umbrella. I have come to know and understand my creator. I have always believed in God, but I didn't follow him, nor did I have an understanding of how to apply God's word effectively in my life. I didn't identify myself with or understand how I had been created in God's image. I am not going to get into great detail—I will save that for my next book—but I began to read many of the books in the Bible regularly. With an in-depth study of God's word, John writes, "Dear friends, let us continue to love one another, for love comes from God. Anyone who loves is a child of God and knows God (1 John 4:7 NLT). In 1 John 5:1 NLT, he writes,

"Everyone who believes that Jesus is the Christ has become a child of God. And everyone who loves the father loves His children, too."

Through my reading, studying, and listening to my heart and others, I realized that my self-image was not healthy and that I believed "who I was not." I had become someone who I had not intended to be, nor did I want to be. I have always felt as though God was on the outside of me and at a distance. When I realized I was not my true self, I said, enough, and I vowed to change my way of thinking.

I began changing my self-image after I understood from where my true identity came, and with whom I had defined it. In Genesis 1:27 NLT, Moses wrote, "So God created human beings in his own image. In the image of God, he created them; male and female, he created them." In a letter from Paul to the Colossians (Colossians 1:15), he writes, "Christ is the visible image of the invisible God. He existed before anything was created and is supreme over all creation." I accepted my new identity, believing that I was a child of God. I am reminded every morning when the sun rises that I am grateful, and I will listen to who God says I am because He is the one who created me, He loves me, and He created me for greatness for His glory. My life has been transformed since I recognized that my identity had been stolen. More accurately, I had misplaced it, allowing the words of others, who they think or say I am, to define my thoughts.

I discovered what I needed to do. I had to listen to my Heavenly Father, accept and believe in who God says He is, who He is, who He says I am, and who I am becoming. Paul wrote to the Corinthians, "That is why we never give up. Though our bodies are dying, our spirits are being renewed every day" (2 Corinthians 4:16). He wrote to the Ephesians, "Instead, let the Spirit renew your thoughts and attitudes" (Ephesians 4:23). Paul wrote (Romans 12:2-3),

"Don't copy the behavior and customs of this world, but let God transform you into a new person by changing the way you think. Then you will learn to know God's will for you, which is good and pleasing and perfect. Because of the privilege and authority God has given me, I give each of you this warning: Don't think you are better than you really are. Be honest in your evaluation of yourselves, measuring yourselves by the faith God has given us."

My new and true self-image has impacted every area of my life in significant and powerful ways. A mentor of mine, Tony Robbins, said, "Human beings absolutely follow through in who they believe they are. We stay consistent with who we believe we are. We define ourselves. It becomes the glass ceiling that controls us." I agree and believe that we need to be ourselves, the true nature of which we were designed, if we are to progress and produce an abundance in life, naturally, and with the effort to raise our standards. We gain momentum through the rituals, disciplines, and intentional habits we put into practice in our daily lives. When we make values and serving others a priority in our lives, our true identities reveal themselves. Our lifestyles should reveal the light and love with which we were created and share it with the world to reveal the light in the world's darkness. I like a quote by Leland Val Van De Wall: "Let us not look back in anger, nor forward in fear, but around us in awareness." It is important to stop old conditioning or beliefs that no longer serve from preventing you from becoming everything for which you have been created, are capable of becoming, or earning all you choose to earn. Author Wynn Davis once said, "Every conflict is a set of opposing ideas. All of us have had the feeling of knowing what we should do on the one hand and doing what we feel like doing on the other. By understanding the two opposing forces warring within us, we come to a knowledge of the truth: we no longer remain slaves. A clear understanding will make us masters." We must all begin to view conflict and challenges in life as opportunities for growth in our character and spiritual lives. Make it a point to see and remember the importance of your self-image and come to know the power brought about by knowing your true identity.

BIOGRAPHY

Devon Kurz has used personal and spiritual growth for great success in the construction and remodeling industry. He is currently investing time and energy building a business through work ethic and word of mouth. He is excited to serve and help those who are working for and looking to get what they truly want in life. He is excited to lead anyone coachable to the top of their careers. Devon spent over forty years in rural Nebraska. He has two children who are now young adults. He currently resides in Oregon.

Contact Information
Facebook: https://www.facebook.com/devon.kurz

CHAPTER 11

MILK AND HONEY

By Dominika Blum

When I was three-and-a-half-years-old, in November of 1978, my mama and I were at a clinic in Warszawa, Poland, returning a strut device that had been attached to my hips and legs for the previous eighteen months. I had been delivered with forceps and a vacuum due to a complicated birth. I was born with damage to the central nervous system, head deformation, hydrocephalus, stretched sternoclavicular and mammary muscle, hypertrophic pyloric stenosis, and hip dysplasia. The hospital released me as a child from the "risk" group because there was nothing they could do for me.

Nowadays, doctors recognize such conditions and have x-rays readily available if needed. Back then, in communist Poland, one could wait up to three months to do a simple x-ray. Doctors did not want to give referrals to see specialists as they believed their own knowledge would suffice. Thank God, my mom was determined to heal her baby. We traveled all over Warsaw on a bus to find experts who would help so she could get me the aid critical to my wellbeing. Though she went through hell and back in the first few years of my life, she didn't give up. She was the one who taught me determination and resilience, and for that, I will be forever grateful.

After we returned the leg braces, we had to get my three-year-old leg muscles strong again. Mama got me a tricycle so I could ride around our tiny apartment to exercise those little legs. As my body got stronger, I went from tricycling to walking, running, and dancing like no one was watching. I sang, and I danced everywhere you could imagine. Mama signed me up for all types of dance classes at our city's Dom Kultury (House of Culture). Since then, dancing is one of my favorite things to do, and I often dance in my kitchen or anywhere, really. The feeling of great rhythm flowing through your veins is one of the best things in the world, and it's an invigorating mood changer, too. Spiritual teacher Eckhart Tolle believes, "Life is the dancer and you are the dance." I couldn't agree more.

Eleven years later, on May 3, 1989, riding in a yellow cab from O'Hare airport to Jefferson Park was a ride I will always remember. Everything was so big. The cars were long and wide. The highway had so many lanes, and the taxi driver spoke in a funny language I did not understand. Everything looked so different, so alive and fresh. The air smelled of limitless possibilities. Because of my Polish-American stepdad, we moved to Chicago, Illinois. The United States of America. The greatest country in the world. The country of milk and honey, the land of the free, where everything is possible.

I was excited about the move, curious about the unknown, and eager to embark on this new journey. I knew it would be hard, but I did not expect it to be as hard as it turned out to be. Late nights of studying became the norm, as did learning a new language, memorizing the words, the grammar, the slang, and the "in-words." Learning and understanding the United States Constitution and history to fulfill my eighth-grade requirements without being fluent in English was challenging. The Internet and online language courses did not exist at the time. There were no smartphones and no apps to teach word pronunciation. I treasured the daily disciplines my mom taught me as a child. The belief that I could learn a new language, that I could achieve greatness, grew stronger. I had no other choice. If it was meant to be, it was up to me.

The first year in my new world was one of the hardest in my life. I cried myself to sleep most nights, but to thrive and not just survive, I had to rise above it—rise above being made fun of and bullied at school, rise above my cruel school mates. Rise above it all. We have to persevere to succeed in life. One of those successes was when I earned 97% out of 100% on my US Constitution exam.

Success. /sək'ses/ Noun, the accomplishment of an aim or purpose. To succeed, one has to know exactly where one is going, have a clear vision, put in a continuous effort, believe in yourself, do the right thing, be consistent, have grit, be grateful, and, most importantly, love what you do. When you love what you do you will not work a day in your life. Success starts with daily habits and discipline. The only place success is found before "work" is in the dictionary. We can't expect to succeed if we don't put in the work.

My mentor taught me to win the day, every day. Every day do what you can control. Do not worry about or waste your time on anything else. Just focus on what you can do right now. Focus on what you can do today. Ask yourself, what can you do right now to start achieving the goals you have in your heart. Start with the end result in mind, see the prize, and pay the price to get what you want. Envision exactly where you are going, have a plan, and work that plan. Make decisions based on faith and not fear. Henry Ford once said, "Whether you think you can, or you think you can't, you're right;" do your part, and God will do His.

After high school, the question wasn't if I would be going to college, but which college I would go to. I went to one of the best universities in the nation for my major, and I graduated with honors and a Bachelor of Architecture Degree. One year later, I realized that being an architect was not what I wanted to do with the rest of my life. I wanted to change lives. I wanted to travel the world and embrace all of the life experiences I could. I did not want to be stuck in a traditional nine-to-five, and I started to look for a way out. I answered an ad in the paper with the headline, "Airline Attitude!" I had found it. I was so excited! This was my first introduction to working in sales, which was a highly competitive and flexible environment, and I loved it. I loved helping people. I loved the numbers game. I loved the pursuit. I loved the excitement of it all.

My work was based on commission pay only, and not all months were as lucrative as the one before. I started waiting tables part-time as another stream of income while I figured out the sales game. Man, oh, man—did I get an earful of OPO (other people's opinions). Note to self: never listen to anyone who does not have what you want—this applies to all aspects of life—relationships, money, health, wealth, lifestyle, education, experiences, and the like. If we buy someone's opinion, most likely we will end up buying their lifestyle. According to experts, the average toddler hears the words "no," "don't," or "can't" four hundred times a day on average. It's no wonder we don't always believe in our own abilities, as we are trained our whole life not to.

I was twenty-five-years-old, and for the first time in my life, I was introduced to the idea of personal development. "What do you mean we have to work on our minds?" I asked my mentor. The concept was so foreign to me. I then realized that I already had everything I needed to succeed. I had the control to make my life what I wanted it to be, and it all started with what I fed my mind. I began to read good books like *Think and Grow Rich* by Napoleon Hill, *The Magic of Thinking Big* by David Joseph Schwartz, *The Power of Positive Thinking* by Norman Vincent Peale, and *The Power of Your Subconscious Mind* by Dr. Joseph Murphy, to name a few. I nourished my mind with positivity through good books, CDs, workshops, seminars, affirmations, positive self-talk—whatever I could get my hands on—every single day. Our brains are like gardens—what we feed our minds matter. What we focus on expands. Ask yourself, are you feeding the flowers or the weeds in your mind's garden.

Over the last twenty years, I have invested a lot of time, energy, and money in my personal growth. The best investment one can make is in one's self, after all. We all need to work on ourselves every day. Just like taking a shower or a bath, we need it daily. Work on your mind muscles daily. This is a lifelong process. The minute we think we know everything there is to know, we go right back to where we started. Be intentional with who you include in your circle. We have the choice to surround ourselves with positive, loving, driven, goal-oriented people who will uplift us and push us to be and do better, believe in us, and tell us the truth. We must seek out action-takers, powerhouses, go-getters, leaders, achievers, doers, kind, selfless people with huge hearts. I choose to learn and broaden my horizons on a daily basis, using that knowledge in my life. I don't believe that knowledge is power; I believe that knowledge combined with action is power. We can be the most educated people in the world, but if we do not do anything with that knowledge, it does not matter how much we know. To get what we want in life, we must ask for what we want and not what we don't want. Most importantly, what we want must be backed up with love and action.

Ralph Waldo Emerson once said, "The only person you are destined to become is the person you decide to be." Every experience makes us stronger and wiser and drives us to make the right choices. 2012 was a year of major life decisions for me. I resolved to cut myself off from friendships, relationships, habits, and behaviors that did not serve me positively, and I found my purpose. I love exploring and traveling the world. My mom is my biggest inspiration in this area, as she's the one who got me hooked on traveling and discovering the world when I was little. Travel humbles us by showing us how little space we occupy in the world. It teaches us in the most profound ways, stretching our way of thinking, our beliefs, and our imaginations. Saint Augustine of Hippo described this idea when he said, "The world is a book and those who do not travel read only a page." Creating memories with friends and loved ones across God's earth has an impact that will live in us forever. I have traveled to forty countries and thirty US states so far, creating a life from which I do not need a vacation. I am committed to reading the whole book and taking a bunch of people with me along the way.

One must serve others from the heart and see the world from a place of love if one is to be successful and feel fulfilled. The more we love, the more we get love back. Love is a purpose. It is our true power. It is what inspires us and what changes us. Love is at the core of success. Love is the key to all. "We love because He first loved us," 1 John 4:19. God first loved us, so love yourself just the way you are. Love one another, speak life, not death, into your daily life and trust God to do His work. He has a grand plan for all of us. A part of God's plan for me was to serve in Guatemala. I volunteered at San Martin municipal for the first time in 2015 with the Hug It Forward organization that helps build schools from plastic bottles filled with trash. I immediately fell in love with the culture, the beautiful people, children and their love for one another. The El Chocolate community stole my heart and changed my life forever with their big hearts and warm smiles. I returned to Guatemala three more times and led volunteers from across the world to build bottle schools. I am stoked to go back this year for the fifth time in my life, this time with college students from a local university. I look forward to watching them grow into servant-leaders on this volunteer voyage.

Our attitude and mindset, showing up, being present in the moment, and having the belief that you will win are all a part of victory's bigger picture. My good friend, Roscoe, says that you've got to show up and participate in your own rescue. We all live in a time of abundance, but when we make decisions based on fear, we believe the lie that we live in scarcity rather than abundance. Whatever we believe becomes our truth, turning our perceptions into our realities. Our words are powerful. We speak life or death into our lives daily by what comes out of our mouths. We either build ourselves up or tear ourselves down. It is so easy to be negative, to complain and play the victim. I challenge you to change your way of thinking over the next thirty days and start paying attention to your thoughts and words. When negative thoughts manifest, change them to positive ones. Love instead of hate. Think before speaking. Compliment instead of complaining. Be the victor God made you to be. There is more than enough love, abundance, prosperity, wealth, and goodness in this world for everyone. God gave us dreams and goals for a reason. He sent us into this world not to be in it, but to transform it.

My purpose and mission are to help millions live their best lives. By aligning our actions with our intentions, we can make our dreams come true. It does not matter where we come from. It matters where we are going. Begin by writing down your goals and affirmations and read them daily. Visualize what you want to do and be. Start from a place of love. Believe in yourself, practice positive self-talk and take massive action. Relentlessly persevere daily, no matter the circumstance. Though it sounds cliché, don't sweat the small stuff. Do your part, and God will do His. Dream BIG and go after it. Get your milk and honey, friend. You are worth it.

BIOGRAPHY

Dominika Blum is a sought-after leader with a vibrant and contagious attitude. Best known for her laughter and servant leadership. She is a passionate entrepreneur, speaker, and international advocate for education. Dominika has been inspiring people to live their best lives for the last twenty years. Her mission is to transform millions of people by helping them rise to their highest potential. She believes everyone with the right attitude and mentorship can achieve their goals. Dominika is a life-lover, travel fanatic, dream-pursuer, and relationship-builder. When she's not traveling, you can find her encouraging others, learning, and reading. Her guilty pleasure is ice cream and romantic comedies. She is married to the love of her life, John, the best husband ever. They live happily in South Dakota, USA.

Contact Information
Facebook: https://www.facebook.com/sunattitude
Facebook blog: https://www.facebook.com/UwierzwSiebieDominikazWarszawy
Instagram: https://www.instagram.com/sunattitude
Twitter: https://twitter.com/sunattitude
LinkedIn: https://www.linkedin.com/in/dominika-blum-53046a19
Email: dominikablum@gmail.com

CHAPTER 12

THE MAGIC OF LIVING OUTSIDE YOUR COMFORT ZONE

By Helen Kithinji

I am backstage, surrounded by media production machines and the production team. In the background, I can hear loud hip hop music that sounds like a million people singing along. The auditorium is electric. This extravaganza is making me even more nervous, just as one of the media guys is fixing my mic to go on stage. This is my first time ever hosting an international event. This one is a three-day business training event in Johannesburg, with over 4,000 entrepreneurs from all over Africa in attendance. After my mic is fixed, I ask the production director to give me a couple of minutes to calm my nerves. He didn't need to know that I was going to pray and then telephone my coach. My heart was racing, my palms sweating, all of which was reminding me of a past experience in a similar situation.

I was assigned the role of introducing my singing group during one of our performances at the Conservatoire in Nairobi, back in my high school days. Our music coach Mr. Walshaw had prepped me well. Once on stage, I was to take one step forward from the other 11 singers, introduce the group, then give an outline of the classical pieces that we were going to perform. I'd spent two weeks memorizing my short speech and practicing every step, the pose, and the smile. I had mixed feelings, as we waited for our performance slot. I was feeling excited about the opportunity, yet nervous and scared at the same time. When our time came, we walked onto the stage, formed a neat semi-circle, while the audience applauded. When the applause was over, our music coach signaled me to start. I stepped forward to do the introduction. I could barely see the faces of the audience through the dim lights, but I could feel their eyes on me. The pin-drop silence paralyzed my mind and my mouth. I went blank. I couldn't remember what I was supposed to do or say. I stood there tongue-tied, trembling, staring into the audience like a statue. That one minute felt like five minutes and only ended when Mr. Warshal snapped his fingers from the far end of the stage. Everything streamed back into my mind, and, judging by the applause after my speech, I had done a good job, after all.

The memory of this experience gave me a tremendous fear of public speaking for a long time afterwards. Indeed, when I was working as a public relations manager in the bank where I worked many years later, history repeated itself during a bank-customer relationship event. My boss missed his flight, and I had to host the event. When I stood on stage to kick off the event, my mind went blank again. I remember the sweaty palms, my heart racing, and my whole body trembling. After a minute of paralysis, I gathered my courage and managed to run the day's program smoothly. This was the last incidence of my stage paralysis, but definitely not the last of my stage fright. Over the years, I have had numerous occasions to speak onstage, every time experiencing nervousness and anxiety, especially in the minutes just before going onstage. Today, I no longer have those mind-locks and am more relaxed on stage. Taking training courses on how to be an effective speaker and practicing every time I speak means that I get better each time.

You would think that having spoken onstage many times before, I would be confident about hosting my first international event. After all, the only difference here was the size of the stage, the audience, and the auditorium. I had prepared well, carefully choosing my outfits, accessories, and my hairdo, and I'd practiced my opening speech, researched some stage jokes, and watched videos about emceeing. But here I was, deathly nervous, almost about to back out at the last minute. But my determination to be a highly sought-after speaker got the better of me. I spoke to my coach, who guided me through a centering process. I took some deep breaths, whispered a prayer, and was finally ready to face my fear. As my name was announced, I walked onto the stage, raised my hands up in the air, inviting the audience to stand and dance with me. As I danced across the stage, my stage fright was suppressed. My courage was boosted by the love and energy of the audience. The audience danced along happily, with some people shouting my name and sending flying kisses, fueling my courage and strength. I had interacted with most of the people in the audience in person or through social media. Most had been following my journey, as I built my global travel business, becoming a top thought-leader, and earning a million dollars in commissions over six years in our part-time, home-based business. It is my success in this business that earned me the coveted chance to host this event. My journey to earning a million dollars is one I can summarize in one sentence: "I found my fortune outside my comfort zone." I've found that my growth always comes from pushing myself through uncomfortable experiences.

When I look back at my early years growing up and then as a young professional, I've found that my major achievements were always preceded by intense fear, anxiety, and the temptation to quit. As human beings, we're inclined to try to protect ourselves from the unfamiliar. We tend to resist that which pushes us out of our comfort zone and toward change. Yet it's through change that we grow.

All personal breakthroughs begin with a change in beliefs. That's what I've learned over the years; to make a breakthrough in our personal development, we have to start by challenging our long-held beliefs that were formed during our upbringing and our life experiences. During my early years, my beliefs about success were shaped by my parents and the community around us. For instance, my father was a traditionalist who believed that one only needed to work hard in school and get good grades to secure the ideal—a job with the government. The most coveted government jobs at the time were high-school teacher and district administrative officer because they were seen to provide job security and a modest salary to live on until retirement at sixty.

My observations told me that the majority of civil servants lived peaceful, average, event-free lives, providing the basics for their families, but never really achieving massive success. Because I had bigger dreams for my life, I decided to focus on securing a job with a multinational company or a bank. My father and his generation grew up with the belief that working for the government presented the best opportunities and that it was difficult, almost impossible, to qualify for a job in a private enterprise. After making applications to fifty-three banks listed in the yellow pages of an old directory, I secured a position with the largest bank in the region. Fifteen years later, I exited the banking industry as a highly successful senior bank executive to become an entrepreneur.

Ten years have passed since then, and I have grown into a successful entrepreneur. I run a global business, have invested in a couple of other businesses, including a financial institution, where I serve on the board. I've achieved accreditation for executive coaching and often publicly speak to and train entrepreneurs. I'd like to share the key principles and lessons that I've employed to create a system for continuous growth in all areas of my life, including my health and fitness, parenting, relationships, career, business, lifestyle, and spirituality. Most recently, I achieved the milestone of having earned a million dollars in my home-based business in only five years, an achievement that I never thought was possible.

1. **Identifying and replacing limiting beliefs**

    Personal development and my coaching training exposed me to the power of questioning every limiting belief that stands in my way of achieving my goals. Psychologists have proved that our brains are always trying to move us away from anything unfamiliar or that we think might cause us pain. By asking powerful questions to interrogate such beliefs, you can overcome and replace them with supporting ones. Some of the questions I ask are:

    "How has this belief served me in the past?"
    "How has it limited me in the past?"
    "What will it cost me in the future if I don't act against this belief?"
    "What more empowering belief can I replace it with?"

It's time to get rid of beliefs that do not serve you! Make a list right now, ask the questions, and then commit to replacing them with empowering ones.

You'll no doubt find that limitations will also come in the form of justifiable reasons or excuses. These, too, must be subjected to the same process outlined above. For example, in the past, I told myself that I couldn't go to the gym because I didn't have time. After going through the questioning process, I realized that neglecting my fitness would cost me later in life in the form of medical bills. I dropped the excuses and hit the gym.

2. **Setting high standards**

To create intense desire and drive to achieve audacious goals, I set high standards for myself. During my banking days, my boss was always astonished at the aggressive targets that I set for myself. This practice saw me ascend in my career faster than my peers. I continue to use this principle in my businesses and personal projects.

3. **Commitment to continuous learning and personal growth**

Your ability to expand your mind and commit to lifelong learning is critical to your success. My commitment has seen me get ahead in every aspect of my life. There are three forms of learning, namely; *Maintenance Learning* aimed at keeping you in your current position; *Growth Learning* to increase your skills and knowledge, and lastly, *Transformational Learning,* which contradicts and challenges your beliefs, triggers new insights, and creativity to move you forward beyond that which you believed was possible. You can continue the learning journey through certified training events, online courses, books, and validated content.

All successful people that I know of commit to continuous learning, with most reading at least a book every month. Consider the extreme reading habits of billionaire Warren Buffet, who is reported to read fifty books a year and spends hours reading hundreds of pages of business reports every day. Could this routine be one of the keys to his massive success?

In Japan, they have a continuous improvement system called Kaizen. So, based on my experience and knowledge, I recommend committing yourself to the habit of constant and never-ending learning for growth. This is an investment in yourself that will enrich and enhance your relationships, families, businesses, and communities.

4. **Working with a mentor**

   Finding the right mentor to work with can propel you on your way to success, allowing you to be guided by someone with superior experience and knowledge of your chosen field. It's an effective way of shortening the learning curve and avoiding unnecessary mistakes. Your mentor will help you to challenge any beliefs you hold that may be blocking your way to success and boost your self-confidence, leading to further breakthroughs. Throughout my life, my mentors have played an important part in supporting and cheering me. They've celebrated my achievements when I've been successful; and supported me through tough times, helping me to understand my limiting beliefs and pushing me to overcome them.

5. **Discipline yourself to take action consistently and persistently**

   One of my mentors has always said that success doesn't come easily or quickly, you need to be patient with the results but impatient with taking the right action to take you forward.

My message is: Consciously and consistently push yourself outside your comfort zone in order to continue a positive progression. Learn to notice when your beliefs are limiting you and replace them with empowering ones. Imagine that they are the brick wall that you must crash through to achieve your dreams. Don't let the fear of failure stop you. Overcome the fear by doing what you fear anyway. If you're willing to do what is uncomfortable for you to move yourself in the direction of your ambitions and have the courage to tackle the unfamiliar, even when you have no guarantees for success, you will ultimately succeed. It's part of the process to allow yourself to learn through failure, and trust that every time you fall, you'll get up having learned a lesson that puts you closer to achieving your goals. As Thomas J. Watson, former CEO of IBM, put it, the formula for success is simple— double your rate of failure.

Living outside your comfort zone will bring you heightened levels of energy, passion, and an enduring state of happiness and satisfaction. It is simply MAGICAL!

BIOGRAPHY

Helen Kithinji is a successful entrepreneur, investor, an Accredited Executive Coach, and author of one of the most powerful personal development books published: *Profiles on Success with Helen Kithinji*, which also features other global best-selling authors. An MBA graduate, her story about growing to executive management in her fifteen-year banking career, becoming an entrepreneur, and establishing a multi-million-dollar global business in less than five years continues to provide inspiration and encouragement to others in pursuit of their dreams. She has been featured in leading business publications, including the Voyager Magazine, Business Daily, The Daily Nation, Business for Home, and The Standard newspaper. She has won several awards, her latest recognition being the achievement of a million dollars in sales commissions in her online business. She also enjoys a rich, happy family life with her husband—Ronnie—and their two adorable sons.

Contact Information
Facebook: https://www.facebook.com/rahalinks
Instagram: https://www.instagram.com/helenkithinji/
Website: https://www.helenkithinji.com/

CHAPTER 13

I CHOOSE ME

By Ilioara Ormenisan

Why do human beings give up on things so easily?

Has this question ever come to your mind?

My entire life, I've been seeing people around me give up easily on their dreams and goals. Since I realized that, I've been wondering why that is, why don't they want more for themselves. I can't be the only crazy person wishing for things that may seem unachievable.

I've been surrounded by people saying that they want more money and fulfillment in their lives. Yet, when opportunities come, they seem to be blind to them. It's almost as if they're putting on a blindfold and embracing NO with ease, instead of making more positive choices.

Looking from the outside, we can see that people are usually capable of doing what they want, but they just don't see it.

A while back, I was one of those people asking what my purpose in life is. Sometimes, I'd get frustrated, as I bought into other people's ideas about what life should be. Back then, when I wondered about this, I thought of all the many things I know how to do, like baking, sewing, decorating, handmaking crafts, cleaning, ironing, nail technician, etc. But none of that felt like my true mission in life.

I found myself making negative judgments about myself and thinking in the same downbeat way. I felt similar to the way I did before my husband and I started our relationship. We've known each other for 26 years, but our romantic relationship only started seven years ago. Before we started hanging out, I was single for two-and-a-half-years, and every date I went on was a failure. Plus, all the time, I had the feeling that everything was falling apart. At one point, when I thought about this, I remember thinking that I was sure what was "mine" was waiting for me, but wondering when I was going to find it. I often felt the same about my purpose in life, too.

After all this destructive self-talk, I realized that I wasn't heading in the right direction and needed to start looking at things from a different perspective. What if, for instance, my mission in life was to be happy, spread happiness and joy around me? That could lead to amazing situations. I started to enjoy the little things in life more and began to see the good in people, even the ones who annoyed me. But the most important change I made was to start being more grateful for everything around me—and I mean, absolutely everything.

Have you ever been in a situation where you felt it was right to trust your gut about something and, despite anyone else's arguments, you went ahead and did it anyway?

I surprised myself by acting this way even when my family and friends disagreed with my intentions. But I knew I had to trust myself and take that leap of faith in order to move forward. It wasn't always easy. I have been blessed with challenges, but my intuition has usually proved that I've made the right decision. You might wonder why I say I have been *blessed* with *challenges?* Let me explain: By deciding to change my outlook, I came to the conclusion that every challenge (I stopped calling them problems long ago) I faced in my life could be overcome if I faced it with courage.

I believe this has helped me become a better and stronger person today. I hope you understand the message I'm trying to get across—that challenges are actually *blessings* in disguise. It's not so much about the challenges that we encounter throughout life. It's about how we face them and deal with them.

I am 100 percent certain that every single one of you, at some point in your lives, have come across a situation which, at the time, left you breathless or completely stressed out. Then, after tackling the issue, you looked back and thought that it wasn't really that bad after all. I'm not sure how true this statistic really is, but it certainly feels as though one percent of life is what happens to you and 99% is how you react to it.

Please allow me to share my story with you: I always considered myself an ambitious person, but kind and sweet at the same time. Although I saw myself as a fighter in life, committed to succeeding, and working hard to achieve my goals, I still gave up on things from time to time, which led me to the question we started out with. For a long time, I couldn't find an answer to that question of why we sometimes quit things we've started. Maybe I wasn't thinking about it hard enough? Besides, I could always blame it on human nature—that this is who we are as people, and that we are capable of changing our decisions overnight. Have you ever felt this way, or is it really only me? I don't think so.

People might call me crazy and a dreamer, but I believe in magic, and no one in this life or the next can shake my opinion on that. I always considered myself as having a special something, but never really knew what it was. But now I feel that I do.

Do you know that feeling when people are trying to force you into choosing between two different options? That's not me. I'm not the type of person who makes those kinds of choices. That's not my reality. I'm talking about choices that have a long-term effect on you, like quitting college, a relationship, or giving up on a dream that others say is crazy. Isn't it better not to buy into their points of view, but do what you feel is right? I remember a situation that happened before I went to university: I was in a dead-end situation but couldn't accept it. I had a choice between going to university or staying in a relationship. But I didn't want to choose—I wanted both. What happened was that, by not choosing, as most people would, the challenge of having to find ways to overcome obstacles to having both sent my brain to work. And it came up with solutions that worked. This just proves my point that, when you ask yourself questions, your mind is forced to answer.

I'd like to share another story from a few years ago about this point of view: Three months after I got married, I took the decision to leave my family, my home country, and move abroad without my husband. The reason I did that was because I wanted us to own our own home. To achieve that, we needed money for the deposit. So, I emigrated to the UK to find a job and save up the money for it. If I'd let my family's arguments against going influence myself, I would have stayed at home. But I was determined to follow my instincts that it was the right thing to do, and I would succeed in my aim. Sometimes, thinking logically about something just gets in your way. I thought about the fact that I was going into the unknown, I hadn't even got a job in the UK, but I dismissed any worries.

Instead, I listened to my heart, which told me to proceed with my plan and follow my dream. Now, it sounds so easy when I write about it, but at the time, I remember having days when I felt like the sky was falling in. I had it planned that I'd work for six months, save all the money I could, then go home. Except that, in the beginning, I was told that we needed 5% of the total mortgage cost, but when my husband checked six months later, the realtor suddenly wanted 20% and gave us a one-week deadline to find it or lose the house. Once again, I set my brain to work and looked for solutions to the challenge. This is another example of the approach I take with all challenges. I never accept NO for an answer when it's something I really care about.

The important point I'm making here is that I knew what I wanted and fully committed myself to achieve it. I chose to believe in myself and my gut feeling that my choice was right.

I've realized that when I choose to commit to my deepest and, some might say, unacceptable desires, dreams, or goals, which I believe in with every molecule of my body, other people's opinions can't sway me. When you're committed to yourself, you will never give up doing what you think is right, because that conviction comes from inside you. It comes from the heart, and no one can stop that burning desire. Do you remember hearing stories about mothers saving their children from death by almost superhuman effort? From somewhere, they find the strength to save their child, even if it means lifting a car or breaking thick window glass. The same thing happens with us when we're functioning in that space where we feel our dream, our purpose coursing through every single part of our body. It's your life that we are talking about. It's not something to be treated as a New Year's resolution that you give up on after a few days, weeks, or months.

When you truly decide to commit to yourself, when you take charge of your own life, then it's not important how many followers you might have, it's about knowing where you're heading, following your gut instinct, going with your intuition. You have to trust, have faith, and certitude that, when the time is right, you will succeed in your goals because you know your purpose.

Throughout our lives, we let ourselves be influenced by so many people, by family members, by doctrines, but who's to say that they're right and you're wrong? We tend to be judgmental about our actions and often feel guilty about our decisions. We live life doubting if we've made the right choice. But, what if you can choose to create new and different possibilities? Please, would you do me a huge favor? Could you stop living other people's lives and start living your own, in the way your soul truly desires? Don't let yourself be overwhelmed by all this, just take the reins of your life, even if it means breaking out of your comfort zone.

Right now, you might be thinking, *"Pfft! I already live the life I want."* But is that true?

If that's you, then you're not lying to me, you're lying to yourself. Let me give you a tip about choosing—did you know that you can choose to change your reality every ten seconds?

I encourage you from the bottom of my heart to take a few minutes for yourself and take a retrospective look at your life; think about the things from the future you can bring to the present; ask yourself how you really want to live. You can even write down a list of the changes you desire to make in your life. Now is the time to erase all negativity and stop postponing things: It's time to CHOOSE YOU and take control of your life.

BIOGRAPHY

Ilioara Ormenisan is an ambitious, caring, and hardworking entrepreneur. She is creative, persevering, and passionate about traveling. She has a strong desire to make an impact on the world. Her mission in life is to spread happiness, hope, and joy around the world by encouraging others to follow their heart's desires.

Contact Information
Facebook: https://www.facebook.com/ilioaraormenisan
Instagram: https://www.instagram.com/ilioara/

CHAPTER 14

SEVEN LIVING GENERATIONS

By Ilze Strauta

At present, seven living generations span across the planet. These generations are seven distinct groups of people born within a defined period who shared similar cultural traits, values, preferences as they aged, and therefore have similar ideals.

Different countries have different generational definitions based on major cultural, political, and economic influences; however, here are general cultural generations.

1910–1925: The Greatest Generation
1926–1945: Traditionalists or the Silent Generation
1946–1964: **Baby Boomers**
1965–1979: **Generation X**
1980–1995: **Millennials or Generation Y**
1996–2009: Generation Z
2010–Present: New Silent Generation or Generation A

Though it is easy to fall into overly generalized stereotypes when talking about generational differences but each generation's future is affected by its childhood, the outcomes of different childhoods are similar to the experiences and outcomes of history and the future. Every generation has a set of needs, values, and dreams. However, historically each generation holds some bias against another.

People in different countries were influenced by different events, politics, and social life. Due to rapid technological evolution in some countries, people could accomplish and cultivate culture and social life faster than in other countries. It is all the more crucial to consider the characteristic differences of all generations, as today at least four to five working generations are part of the labor market, working together under one roof. This century faces an unprecedented challenge, that is, to prevent misunderstandings between generations, which could lead to unnecessary conflicts. Sooner we understand what drives different generations, sooner we find a way to interact with each other.

How do we find a common language?
Pay attention to the signs of conflicts, controversies, and needless blowouts.

The Greatest Generation

Shortly after World War I, this generation witnessed a new era—stuck between childhood and reality of the war—called Depression Era. The war led to the death of millions of people, destroyed long-established peace and economic stability, and created conflicts between many countries in Europe, Middle East, Russia, Asia, and Australia. This generation became compulsive savers, careful with spending money, and felt responsible to leave a legacy. They grew up to be patriotic and authority-abiding citizens.

The greatest generation lived without the aid of technological advances, like airplanes, radio, TV, refrigerators, electricity, and air conditioning. The concept of "retirement" was alien to them; you worked until you are dead or cannot work anymore. Divorce was a taboo, and relationships were forged for eternity.

This generation experienced not only technological and medicinal change but also a huge culture change.

Traditionalists

Postwar, this generation was surrounded by darkness, doubts, and everlasting concern, but it was at the helm of new work and business opportunities.

Peace, jobs, suburbs, television, rock 'n roll, cars, Playboy magazine, and the Korean and Vietnam War—were few of the defining moments for this generation. Women stayed at home, looked after children, and waited for their husbands to come back from work with a hot dinner. While men worked for one employer their whole lives and provided security and comfort for their families, this generational believed family to be a sacred and eternal entity (meant to be together forever), while children born out of wedlock were not accepted by society.

This generation earned and learned to save money. They planned for retirement, to make up for the hard life after the war. They have been financially prudent, the richest, most free-spending retirees in history.

Baby Boomers

Born after the war, baby boomers are part of the generation when the attitudes, behaviors, and society, in general, were rapidly changing. They were born to work, to be employees, and to be careful and patient. They are very loyal and reliable.

In Europe, after World Warr II, the society experienced a postwar economic rise. In Russia, people underwent various side effects of socialism and collectivization. The United Kingdom faced an economic crisis. In the United States, while many people served in the military, the country's economy was still in better shape. With the advent of industrialization, manual production shifted to machine production, and manufacturing companies provided jobs. Baby boomers worked to secure their children's lives.

Self-righteous and self-centered—too busy for neighborly duties yet strong desires to reset and change the common values for the good of all—this generation became workaholic. Baby boomers are liberal and modest; they were not a part of the labor market but were loyal to one employer their whole lives. They are well-suited to be a team player and oriented toward collaborations. Working with one employer your whole life was considered to be honorable.

Baby Boomers' spending habits and consumerism fuelled world economies. They became famous for spending all the money they earned. Spend now, worry later, buy it now, and use credit— they are not adept with finances. After the war, several planes were converted into passenger planes, which enabled Baby boomers to travel and experience and see more than their parents ever did.

Generation X

Acquiring education and climbing the career ladder are important for Generation X. They look for opportunities, are result-oriented, and focus on self-development and independence in their private lives and financial matters. Not only are they profit-oriented, but they also love to work and live for themselves. In professional spheres, Gen X is motivated by recognition, trust, career advancements, and financial rewards. Followed by baby boomers, they learned to find a balance between theory and practice. They witnessed the fall of the Berlin Wall, the collapse of the Soviet Union, spent most Saturday nights at a disco, MTV, microwave ovens, color televisions, video games, and personal computers.

Often called "lackey kids," both their parents worked. Consequently, this generation is typically independent and does not thrive on micromanagement, and can even be considered entrepreneurial. They focus on saving the neighborhood, instead of the world. They are tech pioneers because they saw the transition from the industrial to the digital age and had personal computers, microwave ovens, and video games at their disposal.

Gen X is not the core advocate of the government. They suffered from the increasing drug problems in schools, mindlessly used credit cards, craved high status in the society, and blindly chased money.

This group desires to achieve a higher quality of life and prefers lifelong learning and earning opportunities.

Generation Y

This generation experienced the 9/11 terrorist attack, internet era, cable television, satellite radio, 2008 financial crisis, the extreme effects of climate change, Google, Skype, PayPal, Facebook, and so on.

Pursuing passion and following interest in work took precedence for this generation. They accept difficult tasks as a challenge and are not too loyal to the employer. They want to work for themselves, and they regularly change jobs to gain financial advancements. They prefer to work in a team, expects leisure time, and can be confident yet aggressive. Growing up at the beginning of the technological globalization, they know everything about everything.

They are ambitious and have a flexible work schedule and an interesting life. They expect regular feedback from their managers, and if they feel unappreciated, they don't shy away from changing jobs.

They grew up as skeptics, but they are energetic, go-getters, and have leadership instincts with built-in self-confidence. With the technological advantage and great digital skills, Generation Y refrains from participating in a "rat race" but works hard like all previous generations. Work-life balance is important for this generation as most of them came from unhappy, divorced families, and saw their parents working two jobs.

Generation Z

Generation Z seeks freedom and self-awareness. They believe in the joys of work and leading a happy life. They carve their lives around the 24/7 principle. They expect challenge and trust at work; are realistic and individualistic. Workplace safety is important for this generation. They are self-starters, confident, and value-oriented. They are known to find new ways to make money and gain fame and profits rather efficiently. They are fascinated by dynamism and are prime multitaskers.

YouTube has come to aid for this generation. They are realistic and understand that no employee can become a millionaire. They learned early in life that time is precious. They are not afraid to take responsibilities or be in leading positions, but they separate private and work life. Gen Z is uncompromising when it comes to working on weekends.

At present, Generation Z occupies a small part of the labor market, but they are very technologically oriented, fast learners, and adapt quickly. They are accurate and creative and eager to be financially stable. They harvest information off the internet.

Their lives are built around and blended in smart devices, modern technology, internet, social media, Facebook, WhatsApp, etc. They are adept in online business techniques, like email marketing. However, their self-worth is often based on the "likes" received on social media, which makes them sensitive to criticism.

However, they appreciate working with experienced colleagues. As most of them still are students, and only the future will show what to expect from Generation Z.

Generation A

Generation A or "digital babies" are exposed to advanced technology from birth. They are born in a fast-changing world with an abundance of information. They are technologically literate from birth and would be experienced in the use of touch-sensitive or artificial intelligence-enabled devices.

Although some parents might be against allowing their children to use technology or limit its usage, such restrictions are of little benefit. Most schools are rushing to transform their teaching methods and incorporate digital technology. It might seem like a clip from a dystopian movie, but this world is the new reality where the new generation is dependent on technology.

Perhaps in the future, Generation A will realize the power of human interaction and the need for emotional attachment.

Bottom Line

Age is just a number, and technology advancements are part of our lives. I am looking forward to more development leading to more exciting opportunities.

If we shut ourselves to new possibilities and don't want to understand and accept changes, the conflict will be knocking on our doors. Had we followed "New way is not a right way," or "Nobody has done it before," humanity would not have progressed. The invention of the light bulb was not a touch of the devil, but the persistence of mankind toward a major advancement of the civilization.

The amalgamation of the work of all generations has led us here. Everyone's work is meaningful, and for that, we must be grateful to each other. Everybody expects a decent salary; a leader who listens and respects their point of view; support from others; and to lead a stress-free life. This is the basic expectation, not a stereotype.

Every generation brings in this world their own set of values and views, motivations, and attitudes. Different people and generations make life interesting. So, do not let life escape from you.

BIOGRAPHY

Ilze Strauta has studied psychology, marketing, entrepreneurship, restaurant management, art, and history of art in Latvia and Russia. She has learned, mastered, and practiced network marketing, social media and digital marketing, and business in the United Kingdom, Europe, and the USA. Strauta worked in hospitality for twenty-four years, before venturing into writing. She has experimented with several occupations: secretary, restaurant manager, event manager, human resource manager, brand host manager, and regional training manager. She considers mentoring and coaching people, who struggle to step up, her favorite passion. Strauta loves to travel, explore different cultures, local cuisines, and meet interesting people. She believes that her Latvian sense of humor has helped her to overcome the challenges of life gracefully.

Contact Information
Facebook: https://www.facebook.com/life.travel.success
Instagram: https://www.instagram.com/life.travel.success/

CHAPTER 15

ACHIEVE WHAT YOU WANT

By Iréne Wrigstedt

My story is my legacy to my children and grandchildren. I hope it will give them the courage to believe in themselves, follow their dreams, and achieve what they want in life.

I want to encourage people who face challenges and think that they lack the ability to dream big.

Everything is possible. Don't let negative thoughts limit you and don't listen to negative people. Determine what you want, express it, and embrace it courageously when it shows up. Go with your gut; it knows what's right for you.

I always have dreams. I am not afraid to fail. The goal can always be amended.

It's not that I don't listen to other people—I used to do it a lot and followed what they said even if I didn't agree. I stayed quiet to avoid conflicts.

I grew up as a lonely child with loving parents. I was their everything, which turned out to be a significant burden. Everything should look good. My father once told me I was *a good average person*. It has followed me to date. I developed a self-image of not being good or intelligent enough. I imbibed it and lived the first part of my life in the shadow of that perception.

Even though it felt lonely to grow up without siblings but not having anyone to lean on or get help from has made me strong.

Due to the experiences growing up, I made it a priority to be kind, loving, and caring toward others. I try to support and help my children and friends as much as I can.

I value honesty, love, trustworthiness, and ethics. As long as you are brave and have faith, success will follow.

I always did things outside the box even before I knew the expression existed. People often laughed at me and criticized me. I think it says more about their insecurity than about me.

Money and creativity drives me. Growing up, I experienced a lack of money; my parents were open with me about our financial condition, which made me anxious. Later in my life, being totally broke taught me the value of money. It became my goal to build financial security for my children and me.

Creativity is also an important factor. I love nurturing ideas and developing them into businesses and help people grow.

When I was twenty, I moved to Lausanne to work. My parents repeatedly warned me that it would not be possible to find a job and a place to live. But I was determined. I had been studying there after the gymnasium and had a great time studying, partying, and skiing. I moved, got a job, a flat, and continued the fun life.

After two years, I was ready to move back home. I wanted to buy a horse. Ever since I was little, I was horseback riding, so it was a long-due wish. Due to the cost involved, my parents did not support me, but I had saved enough to buy a horse.

Even though they did not support me initially, my parents did not shy away from boasting about me coping so well in Switzerland and back home my participation in horseback riding in front of their friends. That did hurt me as they did not support me from the beginning.

I was raised as a good family girl, always conditioned to do the right thing. I was trained in how to *behave* in various situations. I did not understand why it was important and of what use. Despite all this, I did my own things.

All this amounted to making me feel prestigeless, which I see both as good and bad. Good because I don't care about prestigious things, and I am not afraid of being embarrassed. Bad in a sense that people might perceive me as having no courage or impact.

Being prestigeless does not mean that I don't own prestigeful things such as nice clothes, nice cars, and a beautiful house. I have decided to indulge in these luxuries for my pleasure and happiness, not to gain validation from others. I am not boastful, just grateful though I have experienced jealousy, which came as a surprise to me.

I have never been jealous. I take full responsibility for my actions and for what I have achieved, and I am happy for other people achieving success.

I was asked to go in therapy by my husband and my business partner to become more easy to manage. So I did.

I also did some massive life coaching at Landmark—making up with your past and creating your future. It changed me as I gained insights about myself and was given tools to make changes if I wanted.

I asked for a divorce from both my business partner and my husband.

After moving back from Switzerland, I started working as a secretary to the CEO, something my parents had encouraged me to do. I served coffee, took shorthand, typed out letters, and behaved kindly. I performed well, but my bosses were still unhappy as they could not *master* me. So, I took a degree in marketing and started a new career.

In 1992, I saw an opportunity to set up a business based on a concept that did not yet exist in Sweden. The timing was right, and the market was there; I hit the ground running. I also brought in a business partner. After a few years, I expanded the business to Denmark, Norway, and Finland. I had seventeen offices in four countries with around three-thousand people on the payroll.

As I was still living with the self-image of *a good average person*, I did not assert complete authority in my business. I relied on my business partner too much, who prohibited me from talking to our staff because I did not do it the right way, and they were afraid of me. I believe that it was my business partner who was afraid of my success.

While in the business, I gave too much authority to the senior managers, which resulted in me losing control of the company.

At a turnover of a hundred million Swedish crowns, I filed for bankruptcy in four countries due to the lack of control. I also found out that people whom I trusted had cheated me.

I ended up broke. I had built a big company, helped my clients earn a lot of money, and given my employees good salaries as I appreciated their work. Everything fell apart in a few days, and no one had anything good to say about me. I was left with absolutely nothing.

As my clients were well-known, the media in four countries started to chase me to dig scandals and sell stories about me. There was nothing to find, but they were dealing with a naive person with a lack of control, so they started to concoct stories. It was an awful experience.

Despite the downfall, the business idea was still fresh, and the market was still responsive. A businessman saw this as an opportunity and stepped in to earn money. I was very vulnerable and did not object as he put a good plan into action. He decided everything and I just followed. For me, it was good. We reopened in Sweden and I moved to London to continue the business I already had there. After a few years, our partnership came to a bitter end and we sold the business.

This gave me some money, and I went on doing what I always thought was cool—living on a beach in a beautiful sunny place. I moved to Barbados and started a Jet Ski rental business. I soon realized that life on the beach was the same as in an office and had similar problems.

So when the person with whom I was testing a business idea in France six months ago called and informed me that our client wanted to roll out and wondered from where I intended to work. I realized I needed to go back and pursue the business that I was good at. Luckily, I spoke French.

I spent ten years in France, and we built up a big company. We designed our own offices—a 750 square meter wooden building with central heating and rainwater harvesting system. A wooden, ecological building led to a lot of media coverage.

After being away from Sweden for fifteen years, I wanted to move back. I missed my children and grandchildren. So, I sold my part of the company.

It might seem like that everything has been easy, but that's not the case.

Almost everything I have done received criticism. I often ask myself where I got the courage to go after what I want, bearing in mind the people who tried to stop me. I think I am naive. I express what I want. I do not see the obstacles, or if I see them, I do not let them decide my course.

For instance, when I moved from the outskirts of Stockholm into the city, I wanted to live on the street where my mother grew up because I have nice memories of my childhood with my mother and grandparents. I wanted an apartment there with a terrace. This street has old buildings with no terraces. People told me that I would never get one. I found my apartment with an eighteen-square-meter terrace.

Another time when I lived in London, I wanted to live by the sea. I had lived by the sea for a short period in Barbados, but I wanted the same in Europe. I just did not know where and when.

I met with my French business partner at a convention in Paris. He saw my specific skills and asked me to set up a company with him. He lived in northern France by the sea. So my flat happened to be just a few meters from the sea.

While moving back to Sweden, I decided to live in the village where I spent my summer holidays ever since I was a one-year-old girl and I have many pleasant memories. I wanted a land by the lake. But there was no land to buy by the lake. It did not exist. I was determined and kept expressing my desire, and after a while, the real estate agency called and showed me a land—by the lake.

I designed my own house with an indoor swimming pool that has always been my dream. I received several negative comments about how difficult it is to have an indoor swimming pool. Ironically, from people who never had one.

Today, I live in a nice house by the lake, and I own my dream car—a Mercedes convertible. I have a dog—a lovely five-year-old Rhodesian Ridgeback—that I always wanted, gifted by my son.

I am grateful for what I have. I have it because I have been brave. I have always expressed what I wanted. I have not let the negativity affect me nor listened to the naysayers.

I have gone through difficult times, filed for bankruptcy, two divorces, raised two children on my own, and an ex-husband who committed suicide. These challenges never stopped me.

I now look forward to my new career in the network marketing business, which is a new experience for me. When I moved back to Sweden, I wanted to learn something new, meet with new people, and undergo new experiences.

A friend introduced me to the possibility of earning money in a new and exciting way by leading, cooperating, and helping other people to succeed together with me. I have just started this exciting journey, and I am determined to succeed.

Here is my advice:
- believe in yourself
- do what you want to do
- follow your gut feeling
- don't seek all answers in the beginning; eventually, they will show up
- don't be afraid of failing
- be brave and take opportunities as they come
- don't pay heed to negative people
- don't believe everything you see on social media
- base your decisions on your own experiences
- don't harbor preconceived opinions; look for facts
- be kind, helpful, honest, ethical, loyal, trustworthy, and loving
- be persistent—it takes time to build something stable

It is not always easy, but I keep working on my life every day.

BIOGRAPHY

Iréne Wrigstedt is determined, stubborn, and does not mind the obstacles, which has led to achieving her goals. Iréne wants to encourage others to dream big—express your goals, believe in yourself, be brave, and you will get what you want. She writes about life experiences and the consequences of her decisions and actions. Iréne has been a self-employed entrepreneur for thirty years. She introduced new market ideas, built companies in six European countries, had thousands of employees, and helped hundreds of clients to make money. She has made mistakes and failed. But this didn't stop her, and she continued working on new projects. Iréne lives in Sweden. She has two children and grandchildren who are precious to her. She loves her long daily walks with Khathu, her lovely Rhodesian Ridgeback. She plans for a new career in network marketing, along with playing more golf and dancing more salsa.

CHAPTER 16

REACH

By Joan Kenyon-Woods

From my humble beginnings in Jamaica, West Indies, I understood the concept of hard work. As a five-year-old child, I remember caring for my aunt's and uncle's children. I had chores, too, like fetching water from a huge well. There was always the possibility of falling in and drowning, but that thought never crossed my mind because I was given the task of fetching the water for cooking or washing, and I had to complete it. Young, old, everyone became adept at gathering water from that well. Being expected to contribute along with everybody else taught me the value of family, community, hard work, and what it takes to succeed.

We left the idyllic countryside of Jamaica and immigrated to England when I was about six years old. I was enrolled in school, which was not such an ordeal, as I was already accustomed to the British education system that the Jamaican schools had adopted. However, I was not prepared for the class that I was placed in—I was in the third class from the bottom. It was a system that tracked students into homogeneous groups. The school was called Copland, and the classes corresponded to the name, with C being the highest and D the lowest. I was placed in A, the third from the bottom. As I languished in that class, I was acutely aware that I did not belong there. I felt smothered and lost. My constant thought was that there had to be more than this. I knew I had more in me, and I wanted more. I suppose I manifested what happened next.

I loved sports and excelled in track and field. I always gave my all and was very competitive. I could run faster than some of the boys in my school. The British love sports, and track and field is popular. I ran track, and I also played a game called Netball that is the female equivalent to basketball, except you can't move once you have the ball, but only pivot. The objective is the same—you score by getting the ball through a netted hoop. I loved sports because it created a level playing field for me. What I seemed to lack in the classroom, I made up for on the sports field.

For my parents, being in class 7-A, the third from the bottom, meant failure. Like Sisyphus, it seemed that I was rolling the stone of my high school life up a hill destined to have it roll back down into this dead-end of a class. However, belief and a great attitude can change everything.

It was sports day; my time to shine! It rained—that's England, but I was determined that it was not going to rain on my parade. I had a positive attitude and upbeat spirit, though I do not know where it came from. Although, I have to say, my parents were happy people. My dad always made jokes and wanted people to laugh, and my mom loved to laugh.

That sport's day, the gym teacher left the playing field and casually said, "Joan, you are in charge," as teachers did in those days. Nowadays, you dare not leave a class or students to their own devices. It is a recipe for disaster. But, that day, something switched on inside me, like a light bulb coming on. I rallied my team, and we took on the biggest and the toughest.

Although, the tough kids were not going to succumb to the authority of another kid. So, it was a scrappy game. My nemesis, who shall remain nameless, dropped the ball, which I promptly kicked—only to have it hit her right in the face. To say that I thought I was dead meat is an understatement. I had one recourse, she had to catch me first. I didn't have time to think, I just started to run. I knew neither she nor anyone else could catch me. And she didn't. That's the first and last time I ran from a fight. I don't mean a fistfight, hell, I'll run from those every day, but I decided at that moment that I would face life's challenges head-on.

Not long after that, the same teacher—my savior, my mentor, my hero—moved me from class 7-A to 7-C. The challenges of this elevation in life were many. Now, I was required to work twice as hard to get the desired result. The greatest reward, however, was the caliber of people with whom I was now rubbing shoulders. It was as though my whole life had turned around in an instant. I do not remember the people in class 7-A, but, to this day, I have lasting friendships with many of the people in 7-C. What did I learn? I learned about discipline, persistence, and perseverance. My mind expanded and never contracted again. I developed an avid interest in personal development, consuming as many books as I could on the subject; I realized that the world is wide, and I wanted to know how wide. It was not as though everything changed overnight; it took some time to adjust. But adjust I did. I wasn't good at math, so I was in the class below, 7-O. It mattered not. When I was with the movers and shakers, I leveled up. I elevated my thinking, my expectations, and my efforts. The conversations we had, the ideas we discussed, It was as if I was part of a mastermind group. We still have those earth-shattering discussions about politics, relationships, religion, and everything else.

These were brilliant people who I did not know existed until my gym teacher changed my circumstances, for which I will be eternally grateful. I often think of Mrs. Okupa and have tried, in vain, to find her. I remember those little, short, all-white outfits she used to wear, like a tennis player. They were crisp and clean, with precise and well-formed pleats. That was her uniform, and she wore it every day. It seemed as though she must have had hundreds of the same outfit stashed in her wardrobe. I don't remember what part of the continent she originally hailed from, but her African accent was rich and warm, and she exuded a confidence that commanded respect. She was loved by all, but perhaps most of all, by me, because she was responsible for transforming my life and putting me on the path I was to follow. It was Mrs. Okupa who gave me the belief in myself that I have relied on all my life.

Then one night, when I was writing this book and talking to a friend, my phone began ringing. It kept on incessantly, but I didn't answer it—I had that sinking feeling, the one you get when the phone rings late at night—it must be bad news. However, when my aunt, who lives in Canada, and my cousin, who is usually asleep by 8 pm, kept on ringing, I knew it must be something serious. When I finally plucked up the courage to answer, it was to learn the news I had been dreading; my beautiful, lively, generous, intelligent, hard-working mother was dead. Alzheimer's is a cruel disease, and she had been suffering from it for a while. The whole family was forced to watch, appalled, as this wonderful woman literally deteriorated in front of us. Of course, despite knowing her death was likely to happen at any time, I was devastated by the news, and the loss was still very painful.

However, as time passed, my initial sense of panic gave way to the remembrance of all the wonderful lessons she had instilled in me. I remembered, when I languished in that dead-end class, my mom always encouraged me to reach a little further, do a bit more, and aim to be more than I was. When I think of my mother, I think only of her successes. I knew there had been failures in her life because my parents were divorced, something which my mother never really got over. However, I also watched her turn that failure, as she saw it, into a resounding success. She was, by all accounts, a workaholic. That was why my mom ended up owning four houses within ten years of us moving to the USA. It was through lessons such as these that she taught me to reach for what I wanted.

When we immigrated to the United States of America, the move could have been far more traumatic than it was, if not for my mom. We had to leave everything behind in London: my dad, my friends, my way of life, even a boyfriend. But my mom made the transition easier, taking us to live with my aunt, who had us all working within two months after our arrival. We arrived in September, and by November, I was working in Macy's, New York. That was a culture shock. We were all living my mom's dream. I would hear her talk on the telephone to my aunt back in London, who told my mom that the USA would give her everything she wanted—and she was right.

The job at Macy's famous department store was my first ever—and turned out to be quite an important one for me. To get there, I had to travel into Manhattan every day on a crowded, smelly, hot train without having a clue how to navigate my way through an equally crowded Manhattan. I worked in the lingerie department, and enjoyed selling the most expensive nightgowns, those I couldn't afford, to the many husbands and businessmen who asked my opinion.

It was difficult getting up in the morning when it was bitingly cold, but I did it because I knew that my salary helped support our household, and none of us could live for free. I was grateful for the strangers who sometimes gave me their seat on the crowded train. It didn't happen often, but when it did, I was genuinely grateful.

In retail, the adage is that the customer is always right. I don't know if the customer is always right, but I do know that you should always be polite towards them at all times. Customers might often seem annoying, irritating, demanding, and sometimes ridiculous, but, in serving them, we must make a conscious decision to respond positively and be as helpful as possible. Although there are times when we would like to give way to our emotions in such circumstances, it's better to remember that the moment we lose control, we have lost control of the situation.

In retail, one learns to practice mindfulness. The ability to control one's response to external events becomes almost a part of one's DNA and can be the key to success or failure. One has to reach inside oneself and regulate one's emotions, and have some compassion and empathy for oneself. By developing this ability, one gradually learns to decrease the reactivity and mood fluctuations that can occur when one lets events trigger and control one's responses.

One practice that has governed my life is remembering to be grateful. Be grateful for the little and the big things. I remember an old proverb, I don't recall the exact words, but the message was: "Gratefulness can transform the common days into thanksgiving; it has the power to transform life's routine tasks into joyful ones and turn opportunities into blessings." As the author Robert Brault advises, enjoy the small things today because, one day, you may look back and realize they were the big things.

Human beings have an infinite capacity for greatness, so what is it that causes us to fear reaching out for that greatness within us? Is it simply that we fear rejection, the knock-backs, or the ridicule of others? As Franklin D. Roosevelt said, "There is nothing to fear but fear itself." But how does one overcome fear? I think it is simply by taking action to do the thing that one fears. Yes, that is how one overcomes the fear. Let me share an example with you from my own life: I was on a trip to some exotic part of the world and was offered a ziplining activity that consisted of three levels of ziplining. I was eager to have a go, but there was a young lady who had accepted the challenge but, at the eleventh hour, became fearful. I was incredulous, as she was already at the top of the fifty or more steps that we had to climb. There were people of all ages there. I was one of the oldest, and there was a young boy of about ten among the group, too.

I began to talk to this young lady and discovered it was her birthday, which is why I assumed she had taken the trip. Now, she found herself fifty feet in the air, ready to zipline across the jungle. She cringed and held back until the last moment. I shared with the group that it was her birthday, and we began to sing Happy Birthday to her. This completely changed her mood— there is something magical about that song. She smiled and laughed while I gently coaxed her into the harness, and she was made to feel secure. I assured her that I would not leave her and even held her hand. Then, before we could exchange another word, she was whisked off over the jungle. I met her at the next level; there were no more jitters or fear in her eyes. Everyone who had arrived before us cheered and clapped for her and, yes, we sang the birthday song again.

BIOGRAPHY

Joan Kenyon-Woods is a motivational speaker, entrepreneur, and world traveler who exudes positivity. Joan has utilized her professions—as a teacher for sixteen years and a social worker for more than a decade—to gain insights into social and emotional responses to life's varied hills and valleys. Joan was a member of the National Speakers Association, where she rubbed shoulders with the likes of Zig Ziglar and other well-known motivational speakers. A wife for over thirty years and a mother of three, Joan is not only a successful businesswoman but also a loyal friend.

Contact Information
Facebook: http://facebook.com/JoanKenyonWoods
Instagram: https://www.instagram.com/JKWoods_love/

CHAPTER 17

UNLEASH YOUR POWER WITHIN

By Josef Buchmayr

Austrians are different. At least that's what people tell me when talking about business. I don't believe it. In my experience, people all over the world have the same dreams, desires, and aspirations with one thing in common—time. Everyone has the same 24 hours a day. It is how we treat these hours that makes all the difference.

Let me tell you how everything started for me. As a young boy, I had big plans. If someone asked me then, what I would like to become as an adult, my answer was straight forward: "I will become a millionaire!" My perspective has changed a lot since then. Today, it's no longer just about creating wealth for myself and my family, but to help others in living life on their terms. To be able to do so, for most individuals, includes having the benefit of time and money.

Most people either have one or none of the two. So how do you get both time and money at the same time? You need to own a business. I'm not talking about being self-employed with no employees—doing all the work on your own. I'm talking about being a business owner and having a system that works even if you're not present.

The moment you find a system that works for you and make the decision to pursue that path, your subconsciousness or inner programming needs to be fixed to unleash your power, live up to your maximum potential, and fulfill your wildest dreams.

You have to recognize that you're worth it, and it is okay to live a life of abundance and have more than those around you who weren't willing to persist and pay the price. You don't have to feel bad or have a guilty conscience if you get the success you always dreamed of.

Let me tell you my story. Even though I had big dreams as a kid, I buried them. Only because a person very close to me told me that it was impossible to become a millionaire if you didn't have your first million dollars in your bank account by the early age of eighteen. As a young boy, this seemed out of reach to me, and that's why I listened to my parents and chose the academic path to prepare myself for a good job.

When I was nineteen, I had my first encounter with entrepreneurship. My father introduced me to two businessmen who showed me a venture they were working on. That day, I envisioned a limitless future and got so excited that I couldn't sleep. I began working, but facing the first few challenges, my enthusiasm wavered, and I quit.

I don't recall exactly, but about one or two years later, a good friend of mine called me and pulled me right back in. We worked on a business venture together and had some initial success. Not long after that, things got tough, and my friend decided to no longer partner with me. This was during our student days. This time I didn't quit, but I stopped putting in the effort necessary to advance one's business and got back to student life. Indeed, it was not much different from quitting.

After receiving a master's degree in Business, I decided not to work for someone else, but to live the entrepreneurial life again. The timing wasn't perfect, as the industry I picked was telecommunication with a focus on landline telephony. I worked hard to establish a business, but the product was going out of the market rather than flourishing. Considering the wrong timing, it didn't take long until I ran out of money and had to get a corporate job. I felt devastated and depressed. I lost faith in myself and felt worthless.

Looking back at my career and the several setbacks I have faced so far, I have realized one thing. The greatest enemy of your success is you. It's your subconsciousness sabotaging your efforts. It's your subconsciously thinking that you cannot be more or have more. It's you subconsciously telling yourself that money is hard to be made and that success is something for people better than you. It's your subconsciously believing that you don't deserve the success you're striving for. This is what held me back for so long. When you finally let go is the time when everything will suddenly come together and move in the right direction.

God has a sense of humor. A couple of years later, after I had established myself at a big international company and started earning a decent income, entrepreneurship showed up at my doorstep again. I met with an old friend of mine whom I hadn't seen in a very long time. He mentioned a business idea that he was now pursuing. This is when I pulled myself up and started a new venture. Only this time while working in a demanding job and having a young family to take care of. I believe God wants to test you and see your true character before he allows the universe to be on your side.

But what should you do if you find yourself in a situation with very little time for a new business? I will give you five steps you can follow.

Step 1: Have a Vision

If you have a good and well-paid job, your family and friends won't understand. Most people, including the ones closest to you, don't believe that an affluent life is possible for them, so why should it be for you (even if you have their best interest in mind). In the beginning, they won't support you, or even worse, they will be against you working on your business. To endure and become successful under such circumstances, you must have thick skin. And for that, you need a *vision*. You have to see the future before everyone else does. You must envision a bright future and imagine all the good that will come with it, for you, your family, friends, and all those you influenced.

Step 2: Make Time

As I mentioned earlier, everyone has 24 hours each day, not a minute more or less. So if time is a constant, how do you make time? The truth is, with the decision to do something new, something old has to go. If you're still spending time watching TV, playing video games, or consuming gossip and negative news, these are things you can easily reduce or get rid of completely. Besides that, you can evaluate the work that needs to be done on a regular basis, like household chores or gardening. You could hire someone to do these chores for you.

If, after that, you still need more time, these are the sacrifices that come along with your decision. Family time and hanging out with friends may have to go as well. You must not neglect your friends (your real ones) and especially, your significant other and children. You have to reach an understanding that is okay for everybody. I, for example, made an agreement with my family that Sundays are family days, which means no work from dawn to dusk on Sundays—*family only*. So if occasionally I have to make a conference call on a Sunday, I have to ask permission first. And if a family trip is planned on that day, the call has to be rescheduled.

One tip here: Open up your mind. Instead of telling yourself that it isn't possible to get any more time, ask yourself, how is it possible? This way, your brain will go to work for you and come up with some ideas. You might be able to squeeze in a call on your commute, or you can meet with somebody during your lunch break.

Step 3: Find the Right Things to Do

Now, as you've found a couple of hours every week that you can devote to your business, you shouldn't waste this time. You must work efficiently on getting things done in these hours as humanly possible. This means no distractions and laser-focused work. But just working efficiently doesn't get you your desired results. You also have to pay attention to the tasks you are performing during these hours. In every field of business, there are a handful of tasks you have to do to achieve results; these are often called income-producing activities. Find out the venture-specific tasks and focus solely on one of these during the precious time you have for your business.

Step 4: Create New Habits

Successful people have one common characteristic: they do the things that average people don't. They don't necessarily like every task they do, but if it is necessary for them to achieve their goals, the temporary pain is well worth the payoff that they've visualized in their minds and are soon to experience in reality.

Whether you like the task or not, to do something you're not used to requires willpower, and this will bring down your overall energy level. If you don't like a specific task, it will require even more willpower and drain your energy faster. There is good news. You can relax here. Push yourself to do the activity for ninety consecutive days, every day without fail, and you will create a new habit. After this period, it will even feel awkward if you don't do the activity even for a single day. But don't try to establish too many new habits at once. Pick one habit at a time; otherwise, it might get too overwhelming, and you might give up before the activity turns into a habit.

Step 5: Persist

Work hard and don't look left or right for at least one year. Have faith that despite all possible difficulties, hurdles, and setbacks along your way, you are on the right path, and everything will turn out fine in the end. Keep on going until the success is yours.

Let me conclude with this: we're all on a journey, and we always will be. And because we are more powerful than we believe, it is our duty to always get better and to march forward and make a difference in the world. So if you ever feel overwhelmed, read this fantastic quote and know—*you're worth it!*

"Our greatest fear is not that we are inadequate. Our deepest fear is that we are powerful beyond measure. It is our light, not our darkness that most frightens us. We ask ourselves, who am I to be brilliant, gorgeous, talented, fabulous? Actually, who are you not to be? Your playing small does not serve the world. We were born to manifest the glory of God that is within us. And as we let our own light shine, we unconsciously give other people permission to do the same."

by Marianne Williamson

BIOGRAPHY

Josef Buchmayr holds a master's degree in Business from IMC Krems, a renowned University of Applied Sciences in Austria. He spent time abroad in Poland and the Dominican Republic. He now works for a big international company headquartered in Vienna, being responsible for risk management in Canada and the USA. Besides that, he is building a business in the travel industry and enjoys helping people to live a life full of fun, freedom, and fulfillment. He loves to spend time with his five-year-old daughter and his one-year-old son.

Contact Information
Facebook: https://www.facebook.com/TripleF.sunshine/
Email: buchmayr.marketing@gmail.com

CHAPTER 18

THE POWER OF FAITH

By Leslie Freeman-Wright

Scotland's national poet Robert "Rabbi" Burns famously wrote a poem—*To a Mouse*, in which he wrote the immortal words (translated from the original Scottish): "The best laid plans of mice and men often go awry." These lines are often quoted even today, perhaps because they contain an eternal truth—even our most meticulously laid plans and schemes are often disrupted—by unforeseen things that happen in our lives. Just when you think you've thought of every detail, drawn up a brilliant, fail-safe plan, and set reminders for yourself, somehow that "thing" you'd set your mind on ends up falling through the cracks. When our carefully laid plans come crashing down around our ears, we often feel that all we want to do is run away, maybe to a quiet beach, where we can forget everything and just listen to the waves crashing on the beach while we drift off into *Neverland*.

That feeling is something I completely relate to. In the early part of 2018, I felt everything I'd worked for, along with my marriage, my faith, and my family were slipping away from me. I had no idea what to do and nowhere to escape to; I was lost. Not knowing or understanding how I was doing it, I woke up every day and went through the motions. At the time, I felt as if I was in some sort of coma, standing back and watching my life crash and burn like a downed aircraft. I felt powerless to act in the face of unforeseen life events.

It began when my father passed in July 2018. Within hours of his passing, I landed a whopping six-day period of hospitalization from a disease I'd never even heard of. As a result, I couldn't attend my own father's funeral. As you can imagine, I was devastated. Life as I knew it was already a whirlwind, but suddenly not having Dad around felt as though everything inside me was dead. Those of you who have lost a loved one will understand this feeling. At the same time, I realized that my marriage was failing, and felt there was no one to turn to share the burden. I was in a complete daze. Just like most people going through such events, I began to realize just how precious and short life is.

Prior to this, I had dreams and aspirations of becoming "someone." Back then, I didn't understand that I was already "someone." I had to dig deep inside myself to find the strength, the motivation, and faith in God's will to make it through the days. Fortunately, my husband and I realized we wanted to save our marriage and make it stronger. We discussed it and decided that we'd create an entirely new marriage. We both understood that no one's perfect, and that we needed to regroup and go back to the time when we initially said "I do" to each other. Part of the problem was that we both have such busy schedules, but we knew we had to work out a way forward and make a decision. That decision was to *work at working* on our marriage. At that point, it was like God tapped on my shoulder and gave me the tools that we needed to rebuild our life together. It wasn't easy, but it was worth it.

You see, I realized that I was placing my faith in all the wrong areas at first. By definition, faith is having complete confidence and trust in someone or something. When I looked closer at my life, I saw that all along, I'd been hoping for different outcomes in most areas of my life, but somehow expected them to occur miraculously, without any effort on my part. I wasn't putting in the work and effort to make the changes necessary to bring about those wished-for outcomes. Instead, I questioned why things, both good and bad, were happening, but never took the time to take a step back and try to understand the reasons for them. However, there came a moment when I finally slowed down and took a breath; that pause gave me the chance to see that everything happening was more significant than me and that I alone wasn't going to be able to change it. For once, I had to make myself believe that I wasn't a terrible person and that my marriage wasn't failing. That horrible feeling of being in freefall, that everything you think you have a hold on is disintegrating, might actually relate to things falling into place. By looking at things from a different perspective, I began to understand that the trials and tribulations I was going through might actually be in my favor. Hard to believe, isn't it? This is when the phrase "with God all things are possible" came to mind, which helped me to understand that the faith factor I was missing was ME. I'd given up on me a long time ago, and it took my world to fall apart for me to look up and see that I believed in God and his faith in me, but I needed to rebuild myself and my faith within if I was going to move forward.

When I sit back and look at every major obstacle that was thrown in my direction during that dark time, I now see it as a period of preparation: Preparation for what was to come and finding the way to getting where I wanted to go. I believe that all things happen for a reason, and light shines on every shadow; I'm here to testify that believing in myself and what I could do with passion and positivity set forth in my life, and a change of mindset is powerful.

With this new insight, I fought for my marriage; I went to individual and joint counseling with my husband. Together we created a prayer wall, read a lot of relationship guide books, and went to a marriage retreat. There we learned valuable life lessons that not only helped with our relationship but also to become the positive role models our two beautiful girls needed. Talk about relationship goals! I'm proud to say that through our fight, determination, efforts, and hard work, we are now one hell of a power couple, and I'm so glad our kids have strong role models to look up to.

Life wasn't easy, and trying to rebuild it from the ground up was a definite struggle at times. There were tears, yelling, breakdowns and the "give up" attitude. I fell victim to that situation where you wake up every day wondering what else was going to happen. Many times, I just wanted to close the chapter and walk away. I wondered how things had got here, where did we go wrong? Yet, at the same time, I had to dig deep, stand still, take a deep breath, and start the day anew, and keep pushing on to find the belief that I'd buried deep inside. One of my sanctuaries was going to my fathers' gravesite. There were days when I'd just park my car alongside the cemetery and cry while playing some of Dad's favorite music. Though he wasn't physically here on earth, he was still there for me. Anytime something new happened in life, good or bad, I'd make a point of going to hang out with him, make sure he was okay, and share my stories with him. Of course, even today, it still breaks my heart that I wasn't able to attend his funeral because I'm sick with a disability that's invisible to the naked eye.

At times I felt angry, questioning God as to why these things were happening to me, asking where did this disease I'm afflicted with come from, and why now. I'm not going to lie; that was by far the most difficult part of my grieving, not being there for my dad. However, as with all things, I know he wouldn't stand for me, NOT getting the proper treatment that I needed. Yes, all of this was going at once, and good days were hard to come by.

But, through these struggles, I somehow managed to find out what a strong person I am. I might have been broken, or so I thought, but I never let that keep me down. Somehow, through the pain and the sadness, I mustered the energy to pull through. I believe staying in tune with myself and the new version of who I wanted to be made all the difference. I refused to let the bad win. I'm a fighter, and I would prevail. Aside from my past and things I couldn't change, I could still learn from what was happening. I learned from my mistakes, so I knew what NOT to do moving forward. I had to fix my mindset and remain as positive as I absolutely could. My energy spilled over into my relationship, and my husband and I began to implement changes, putting into action everything we'd learned over the years, so that our love began to thrive once again. I could have walked away numerous times, but that is the easy way out. Easy for the relationship, but hard for the kids affected by their parents splitting. But again, learning to fight for what you believe in, and letting faith intervene was the blessing that I needed.

What would you do in time of need? Would you take the easy route and walk away, or would you stay and work for a better lifestyle? Would making changes to your daily habits benefit your overall health, both physically and mentally? If they would, how bad would changing your mindset, life, and routines be if you knew the outcome would be beneficial? What if you had no idea what was on the other side? Would you make the leap of faith and believe in yourself to see what the outcome would be?

Everyone has a story, a struggle, a romance, a heartbreak, but not everyone is strong enough to pull through them. Life has a sense of humor where you first get the test, then the lesson comes later. It's kind of crazy how that works. What you don't realize is that everything seems important—until you get sick, whether that's physically or mentally. For it's at such times that you realize what's really important to you. Believing in your self helps you to find a way to keep going and rebuild your life, to leave behind whatever has you stuck.

Most importantly, you'll learn to take care of your health and start to realize that whatever you were fighting against might be the very thing you need to work on to make it right. Sometimes, you just need a moment to exhale, take a good look in the mirror, and realize what you have and what you're working with. If you alter just one thing every day, you'll see what God can do. Believe in yourself, because the power of faith is so strong. If you just believe in yourself, as I learned to do, and alter one thing at a time, your mindset will change, too. My experience proves that all great things happen to those who work hard for them and focus on believing that faith lies within themselves.

To date, my husband is my rock, my confidant, and my best friend. We aren't perfect, but the Lord knows we were meant to be joined as one. Together, we're working towards our future goals and building a proud legacy that our girls can one day emulate. It's all about the right mindset, belief, and faith. You don't have to believe in God. Just remember, if you don't have faith in yourself as a person, then no one else will. There are times in life when you just know that you have to do what your heart tells you, when you decide to take a chance on fulfilling your longheld dreams, even if no one else can see that. Going through these tough times taught me that the power to take control of my own destiny was in my hands— I had a vision, and I didn't want to lose it. Time after time, I faced seemingly insurmountable odds and stumbled, but I reminded myself that I'm in charge of my own destiny, I am a mother to two young girls who need a strong role model, a wise leader, and supporter. If I wasn't healthy both mentally and physically within my relationship, then I was a failure, something that I never wanted to be. I knew that if I didn't make changes and uplift myself to find my own happiness, then I couldn't expect those around me to look at me as a source of strength and positive motivation. We all fall, but it's up to you and the faith you have inside you, to choose whether or not you get up, and how you do it.

BIOGRAPHY

Army Brat turned Army Wife, Leslie Freeman-Wright, tells the story of her life and her journey to becoming an important role model for her family, as well as in her community. Working for the airlines, Leslie travels to many places for training events, learning, and teaching others about the industry and how to become successful. In addition, Leslie has been an entrepreneur for over ten years, stepping out into the world away from her day job, and experiencing other things that life has to offer. She has always wanted to write her own books, and finally found her niche through training others to find their full potential in life. By doing so, she has found happiness by helping others succeed in everything they want and love to do. Leslie has also been an advocate speaker at several training seminars and continues to lead everyone she meets find happiness and success.

Contact Information
Facebook: https://www.facebook.com/leslie.freemanwright
Instagram: https://www.instagram.com/poison3f98/

CHAPTER 19

HOW MOMS CAN CHANGE LIVES AND IMPROVE THE WORLD

By Maria Helena Paulo

I am about to share with you how the worst pain I have ever experienced transformed me into a new and better version of me.

I lost my dad in January 2020 after having lost three of my younger brothers over the previous eight years. It is so painful to lose family and, at the time, I lost focus on everything. I stopped going out with my best friends, which I love to do. I was mentally blocked. I didn't know what to do. I wasn't sleeping enough, not eating, not talking. I had no direction, and I was frustrated.

Being the firstborn daughter, I had to care about my mom and the rest of my family, but I had no energy. Then, one day, I went to Mom's house, and we talked; I found that she was so strong and the only one who didn't need my support. She is so much stronger than me, and I dedicate this chapter to my mom, Luisa.

After around three months of losing Dad, I decided to turn my life around, to renew my life. I started rereading books on personal development and happened to read an article by Sashin Govender, a young millionaire student from Durban,

South Africa. He recommended that I read a book by one of his best coaches, Matt Morris.

I am retired from the banking industry, and since August 2018, I have been doing part-time network marketing to help out my mom financially. In the three months since losing my dad, I had lost almost two-thirds of my earnings and a big part of my team because I was not there to work with them. I had lost all my motivation to do anything, and my level of leadership and authority had deteriorated.

So, by reading various articles, I finally found a book subtitled something like: "I was able to finally learn the secrets of stepping up to a powerful position of authority, and my income skyrocketed!" It was by Matt Morris, who promised to teach me "exactly what those secrets are that almost nobody knows about. One: It's in your hands; this book can take any entrepreneur from beginner to celebrity status practically overnight."

From that moment, it was as though something clicked inside me, in my heart and in my mind. I thought I was dreaming, that it couldn't be real. I even wondered if I was having a vision! So, I decided to purchase the book that promised seven secrets to a seven-figure income, but something went wrong during the buying process.

Then, on 7th May, 2020, I received a message from Matt Morris that said: "Maria Paulo, what happened? I noticed that you tried to purchase my book a few hours ago, but, unfortunately, it looks like your order didn't go through. I wanted to check-in and make sure all your questions are answered."

I thought, my God! How can this be real—a celebrity writing to me!? So, I decided to finish the payment process and purchased the e-book. I downloaded, I read, and I watched the videos and the MLM Masterclass audios.

On 8th May, I saw that there was an invitation in my online mailbox to become a co-author to improve the chances of publishing success. I duly filled in the application form but was not expecting a positive answer, as I was depressed and had no experience in writing.

I had never written a book, but I remember having a strong vision of doing something big for my mom, because if she'd' decided to get pregnant during difficult times in 1956, then I was not going to let her down by failing to answer the call of a millionaire, who was willing to teach me how to win big, just by making a decision. That's another reason for being grateful to my mom, Luisa. Dreams really can come true: I remember being alone in my room when I opened my mail on the 14th of May and listening to Matt in his video saying, "Hi, Maria, Congrats for being selected as part of the team of co-authors."

Again, I did not believe that he was actually talking to me!

Moms produce many successful people, people who are leading the world, millionaires who are positively impacting the lives of other moms and their children. These people are scientists, entrepreneurs, constructors, and healthcare workers. And they do this by merely deciding to be moms, by transforming that decision into action. They've found the "how-to" of it, they are committed to their decision, and they care for their children. They are motivated, they believe in themselves, and they use their power positively.

Finally, I say that the world should thank all moms because, by their decisions and commitment, they can change peoples' lives for the better, so that there are smiling faces all over.

Now, let me share with you how far moms can continue doing big things.

Moms, you know how your children are always watching what you do as an example. As you want the best life for them, you should make sure that they see you doing BIG things.

They don't do what you say, but what you do!

Moms sometimes have to struggle to empower their children, but I say, "Woman, go and have freedom of lifestyle; you're powerful, you do have a better way, so go and show the world!"

Moms should encourage other women to do network marketing, as it's a perfect fit for stay-at-home moms. So, if you're a mom who can imagine and believe that it's possible to become a millionaire, you can bestow freedom and help people.

It's a fact that many women are in business but are not making enough money. One way to start making money is through network marketing, where you make a small initial investment on joining.

In the network marketing industry, there's no age limit, no gender, race, or religious bar, and you don't need a formal education, certificates, or degrees. What you do need is to have a vision, to set up your goals, and surround yourself with positive and successful people.

Moms, what is required is to focus on following the system, on doing what your mentors do, constantly and persistently.

There's only one question you need to ask your customers: Do you want to have extra money? If they say yes, then you close the deal with them, and you earn your commissions by spreading your company worldwide.

Moms, you also need to commit to daily habits, like more time, more freedom, and a lot of money.

Moms, you can and should raise your children, and by doing it, you can transform people, helping them toward better health, wealth, and relationships.

When you feel tired or depressed, you can turn that around and fuel yourself with personal development through seminars, webinars, and reading books.

What I've learned is that we should dream big, think big, and realize that to meet our goals and achieve our dreams, we first have to master our skills. To get the big results you want, you have to put in a lot of hard work.

Another lesson to keep in mind is the old rule of 80/20: only twenty percent of people are seriously working; the other forty percent do nothing; the remaining forty percent do a little. In my experience, it's advisable to foster the discipline of always learning something new to get good results. So, Moms, where do you position yourself within the old 80/20 rule? I have chosen to be part of the twenty percent.

Moms, you should schedule time for exercise because it's good for your health. It may be tough at times, but if you set yourself achievable goals, you will be able to push through, and you'll find it's well worth it. To positively impact the world, you must first improve your self-esteem, be kind to yourself. You don't have to be perfect, but just be the best version of you that you can be. Forgive yourself for your mistakes and protect your mental health. Don't let yourself get lost in a maze of anxiety and fear about things, like the coronavirus, where you don't have all the facts—don't listen to rumor or fake news—get out there and get the facts by listening to the health experts. Then you will be able to forge the best path ahead.

Successful moms start by creating a daily schedule for outdoor time, academic time, home cheers, free time, bedtime, and so on. Moms can create more freedom for their sons and daughters and inspire them through network marketing. Moms have transitioned from working in traditional jobs to building businesses that provide a high-quality lifestyle for their families.

These moms manage their time so that they can be as productive as possible when working from home. They create agreements with kids and spouses that make it much easier for them to grow a business, while still having quality family time. So, again, moms can impact their kids in positive ways, as they build their business by supporting and inspiring them.

I am so grateful for this realization. There are so many moms involved in business, whether working corporate jobs or stay-at-home jobs. Here are some of the solutions to the challenges they face: negotiating agreements with kids, partners, and spouses, traveling together, watching videos together about success stories, or involving your significant ones.

It's critical that your kids see the work that you are doing and the positive results it produces.

Reasons for moms to choose network marketing careers:

1. Moms are looking for flexible hours; you can do network marketing online, via phone, in person, during evenings.

2. Women are usually big supporters of other women and are big on motivating them to succeed, but, in a corporate environment, they often experience fear, criticism, or envy. In contrast, network marketing fosters an atmosphere of love, encouragement, affirmation, and supportive coaching.

3. Spending time around other successful women is exciting and inspiring. After spending time with kids, it's great to have a little bit of time with other moms, but let it be with moms who are both inspired and inspiring and love to have fun while making money.

4. Moms are experts in getting the best value for their money, and network marketing startup costs are generally low. Plus, from your very first sale,

you're already making money.

5. There are no barriers to entry in network marketing, and with moms bringing their experience and know-how from all walks of life, it's the perfect place for them to cultivate faith, improve their level of education and work experience.

6. Moms in network marketing enjoy personal transformation, but also build trust networks, get lots of on the job business training, as well as benefiting from attending workshops and webinars. I guarantee that, within two years in the network marketing industry, you will undergo a personal transformation that will be worth far more than the extra money you gain. The material things you'll gain are not as valuable as the personal growth and sense of fulfillment you'll experience. It's not what you get, but who you become—the best version of yourself.

7. Moms like to lead lives of financial independence where they feel they're making a contribution.

So, you can see that network marketing simply ticks all the boxes for moms looking to improve their own lives and those of their children and families. It's an open, flexible business model that promises rich personal and financial rewards. If you want to learn more, I recommend reading Lauren Kinghorn's book, *7 Rocking Reasons Moms Chose Network Marketing Careers*. All mothers, with their work and personal investment in their children, whether they are in paid employment or not, make a vital contribution to the economy of their country. They represent a huge and important part of a nation's workforce and productivity and are vital to the economy's health.

Therefore, increasing opportunities for working mothers would boost the economy. Coronavirus has impacted the economy, especially for moms working from home, who are stressed about not being able to engage effectively at work. Clearly, this will cost the economy billions of dollars.

With COVID-19, there are pros and cons to stay-at-home parenting.

Pros:
   i. Increase in child's school performance
   ii. The child has less stress and aggression
   iii. Social approval

Cons:
   i. Desire to return to work
   ii. Higher levels of stress
   iii. Social isolation for mothers

I would like to conclude this chapter by encouraging all moms to stay caring and work on themselves, their children, and families for the benefit of the world.

Today, we know a lot more about the great things that great women have done and continue to do; they're businesswomen, family carers, students, professionals, domestic goddesses—and moms!

While we often recognize the significant contributions that women make to society as successful doctors, politicians, and lawyers, as well as in all professional walks of life, their overall contribution to a well-balanced and civilized society through motherhood and caring for others is often overlooked.

To close, I can say all that cleaning work that mostly women end up doing, is essential work because without good cleaning and sanitation everybody gets sick!

There is a light inside each one of us that must be nourished, that needs to be cared for to shine brightly, but sometimes it is overlooked, it has not spoken, it has not loved.

Give it the music it needs to dance; that light is you, it's within you, but sometimes it gets forgotten, yet it's the thing that others most want to see, so let it shine.

If you shine, then you give others permission to do the same. So, always climb up and clean the light itself. Always take care of the light within. Don't hide the light. The world needs you to shine.

BIOGRAPHY

Maria Helena Paulo is 63 years old. She was born in Xai Xai, a small village in Mozambique. She has a Master's degree in economics and has had careers in the civil service for eighteen years and the banking industry for fifteen years. She loves teaching and has spent fifteen years teaching economics and finance part-time at her local university. She retired from the Central bank in 2011 but continues to serve the banking industry as an executive board member. Two years ago, she joined the Worldventures company to travel with family and friends. She loves music, dancing, and helping people. She loves her mom, Luisa, and is married to Candido; they have two daughters—Sonia and Sheila, and are grandparents to two lively boys—Caio and Kizua.

Contact Information
Facebook: https://www.facebook.com/mariahelena.paulo.1232

CHAPTER 20

THE KEY FOR LIMITLESS SUCCESS

By Mike Howren

It was November of 2012 when I received a phone call from an old friend. I can't recall what she said, exactly, but I knew that she was more excited than I'd ever seen her. I do remember that she told me she had something I had to see.

Once she arrived, she pulled up a website on my computer, started playing a video, and I was rolling my eyes within 30 seconds. "Are you pitching me a pyramid scheme right now?" I asked. "I've seen dozens of these companies and presentations, and they don't work. They're a scam and a waste of money. Only the people who join in the beginning make money."

You have probably said the same thing at some point in your life, or maybe you know someone who shared a similar story. I had no exposure to the network marketing industry at the time. Growing up, I was told the key to success was to go to school, get good grades, and find a safe and secure job. So, I went to Kent State University, got my degree in business administration, and entered corporate America. I started working with a marketing company and worked my way up through the ranks over the years. By my mid-twenties, I had become my company's vice-president of sales. There I was with a great job, a great title, and a six-figure income. "Man, I've made it!" I thought, but as the years went by, I took on more responsibilities, which meant more time at the office, more stress, and less time to do the things I wanted to do with the people about whom I cared.

We all know people like that—they make good money, but they have no time because they are always working. We also know people who have a lot of time on their hands, but they're broke. I've always been interested in learning how I could have both time and money. I was at a point in my life where every decision I made came down to two things: could I afford it, and do I have the time to do it? Despite my good job, I was still living paycheck-to-paycheck, was stressed out, and time-broke. I needed a change.

So, back to that day in November. I finished watching the network marketing presentation. Honestly, I only watched it to be polite to my friend, and I had every intention of telling her no. In fact, six months prior, I had actually seen a presentation from the same company and had said no at the time. Well, this time, I was introduced to a very successful guy who became a huge mentor in my life. A mentor—imagine that. I had never even considered seeking out a mentor before. I was too focused on just getting through the week, paying my bills, and waiting for the weekend. That day, he asked me a question that completely altered my path in life: "Mike, how many wealthy employees have you ever met?" he asked.

Now, at the time, I thought that being wealthy just meant having a lot of money, so I responded rather quickly. "Doctors," I said.

He looked at me and said, "Doctors are broke."

I was confused, and I politely asked, "What in the hell are you talking about? Doctors make great money," I said.

"Don't get me wrong," he said, "They might make great money, but they're time-broke. If they don't show up at the hospital, they don't get paid. The person who has true wealth is the person who owns the hospital. He makes money whether he lifts his head off his pillow or not." He then proceeded to teach me two laws of wealth that have changed my life forever:

Wealth Law #1: You need to have multiple streams of income—not multiple jobs but multiple streams. Today's average millionaire has seven.

Wealth Law #2: If you don't find a way to make money while you sleep, you will have to keep working for your money, and you'll end up working until you die.

This was drastically different advice than I'd received growing up. Getting a college education and a good job was all that I'd heard about.

Two things dawned on me that day: one—as long as I was trading time for money, I could never have both; and two—the teachers from whom I'd learned in school didn't have their own financial freedom. How could they teach me about financial freedom if they didn't have it themselves? That day, I made a decision to pay attention to that guy because he had the life I wanted, and that has made all the difference in the world.

I started my network marketing career that day with high hopes and aspirations. I was going to "get rich quick." I learned the presentation and began sharing that vision with my friends and family. Some joined me, but many did not, and my excitement began to fade. The negative tapes started to play over and over again in my head, saying, "You're not cut out for this. You're not the type of person who can have success with this. You have a great job, just focus on that. This is for people who can't find a good job." Months passed, and I was very frustrated and on the verge of giving up. It was then that I had a conversation with my mentor, and he convinced me to go to the company's next major training event. I bought a ticket but reluctantly so. I missed a great friend's wedding, but I knew that I had to figure this out if my life was ever going to change.

That weekend, I saw what the industry was all about, and I fell in love. That weekend, I realized something I saw Grant Cardone post on social media years later:

Everyone should be involved in network marketing.

1. For the personal development
2. For the product
3. For the money

Up until that point, I had the order reversed. I was trying to make a bunch of money, but I wasn't working on myself. I had no clue what personal development was. The last book I'd read was in college. If you don't know, Grant Cardone has built a $1.4 billion empire in real estate, was named the number one marketer to watch by *Forbes Magazine,* and is the founder of the 10X Growth Conference, the world's largest business and entrepreneurial conference. He might have just a little more business credibility than your Uncle Buck, who tells you that network marketing is a scam.

I learned something at that event that changed my entire philosophy in life: your income will always follow your level of personal development; up or down, it will follow. Have you ever heard of someone winning millions in the lottery, only to find themselves broke a few short years later? They did not learn how to become the type of person necessary to earn that kind of money, and it left them almost as quickly as it had arrived. Have you ever seen a millionaire lose all of his money only to become a millionaire again a few short years later? This is due to the self-image these individuals have. A person who is broke views himself as broke, and no matter how much money may fall into his hands, he will spend it until he returns to where his true self-image lies—that of a broke person. On the other hand, a rich person views himself as rich, so no matter what losses he experiences, he will do everything possible to get back to his true self-image—that of a rich person.

We function the same way as a thermostat in our homes. We all have financial thermostats programmed for us, and we aren't even aware of it. Our thermostats are programmed from years of us believing certain things about ourselves. What you believe about yourself is a byproduct of your environment, the people around whom you spend the most time, and the programming of your brain by you and those around you over the course of your life. I wasn't trained on this, not in my entire career in corporate America. Instead, I had to learn the skills necessary for completing my job, knowing that I would be fired if I didn't do my job correctly. My company couldn't care less how I felt about myself—they wanted only one thing: performance.

In the world of personal development in network marketing, my self-image changed. I surrounded myself with people who built me up instead of tearing me down. I read books on personal development and was surprised to find them interesting. These books were drastically different than those I'd read in school.

Network marketing and the personal growth I have experienced has changed every aspect of my life. I've made life-long friends, have created countless memories and had invaluable experiences, have traveled the world, and lived life on my own terms. I've been introduced to a group of peers who have pushed me and made me better. I've had mentorship from some of the most successful people I've ever met. I've become a better leader, performer, communicator, partner, friend, son, brother, servant, and an overall better person. Because of this industry, I've learned how to be a business owner, and I have built a multi-million dollar business outside of my network marketing business. I've expanded my mindset and vision and have created and achieved goals that I previously thought impossible.

So, the next time you get a call from a friend or an old acquaintance who has something he wants to share with you, know this: he is not trying to sell you anything. Instead, he has experienced something that has changed his life, and he thought enough of you to pick up the phone to call you. Answer the call and hear him out. You never know if that one phone call might forever change the direction of your life.

Limitless success is never-ending, and it is available to anyone who wishes to unlock it. The key, however, lies within your mind, and the best way for an average person to access that key is to plug into the system of personal development offered through network marketing.

BIOGRAPHY

Mike Howren is a Northeast Ohio native, traditional business owner, six-figure network marketing professional, and an author. Having grown up in the rust-belt, Mike learned the importance of a strong work ethic. It is this work ethic and discipline that has carried him through the ranks of corporate America, but it wasn't until he started working harder on himself than he did on his career that he started to see a change in his lifestyle. His passions include traveling with his fiancée, Lindsay, and spending time with his family, golfing, and boating. His current mission in life is to teach others and inspire them to live life on their own terms.

Contact Information
Facebook: https://www.facebook.com/mike.howren
Instagram: https://www.instagram.com/mikehowren/
Website: http://www.michaelhowren.com

CHAPTER 21

LIVING THE DREAM

By Richard Denning

Everyone dreams, it's the way God made us. We dream about the future, we dream about how things are going to turn out, the great job we are going to have, the vacations, the big house, great family, and plenty of money. We dream about the things we are going to accomplish, how we are going to change the world and make a difference. All those things can come true if you have the right mindset. If you are willing to do today what others aren't, you will have tomorrow what others can't.

Everyone has their own idea of what it means to "Live the Dream." For some, it means financial freedom or the freedom of more quality time. For others, it's owning their own business, being their own boss, or working at something that they feel passionate about. God has given me a passion for helping other people. That's why I have written this book—to help you to discover what "Living the Dream" means for you. I hope that, after you've read it, a whole new world opens up for you and that you will learn how to dream again.

Before we get into the good stuff, let me tell you a little bit about myself. My name is Richard Denning. My wife is Timberly. We have two children and two grandchildren. I live in northern middle Tennessee, about one hour north of Nashville, Tennessee, in the Fairfield community. I have lived here all my life. I am a fulltime farmer and, over the years, I have raised, cattle, hogs, pheasants, quail, chukar, bird dogs, rabbits, corn, soybeans, wheat, oats, barley, sunflowers, milo, tobacco, and, in 2019, I started growing hemp for CBD oil. I also own a hunting preserve and a ten-acre pay lake. Diversification is key to being successful on the farm. If one or two of the commodities are down, some are steady, and some, hopefully, are up. Farming is a great life, but it takes a lot of hard work—precise planning, guts, nerves, and prayers that Mother Nature will be kind to us throughout the year. Farming is probably the biggest gamble in life. We roll the dice every year. It has been said, "Give a farmer a dollar and he will spend ten." Farmers are probably the most optimistic people in the world.

My entrepreneurship began as a young boy when I started raising rabbits to sell. I would also ride my three-speed bike around the area and pick up discarded coke bottles, then take them to the store and get five cents per bottle, which was pretty good money for a young boy. I bought a lot of Super Bubble, chewing gum, cokes, and peanuts. Some of you know what I mean. I also worked at the high school basketball games for my dad, where I started collecting silver coins. I would trade my money for the coins and one-half dollars. My dad taught high school agriculture for over thirty years, and my mom taught elementary school for more than forty years. As I grew up on the farm, I learned hard work and commitment from both Mom and Dad. But life on the farm was not all work—there was play, too. For instance, Dad built a baseball field where we practiced Little League and Babe Ruth baseball and then played church league softball for several years. We hunted, we fished, and attended church every Sunday. To us, that was "Living the Dream."

I played football, basketball, and baseball all through junior high and high school. I graduated valedictorian. I had big dreams. I had to decide to either go to college or stay on the farm. I decided to stay on the farm. I had lived the dream all through school. Now one chapter of my life was ending, and a new one was beginning. I got married, my wife was going to college, and, for the first time, I had bills to pay, real bills. I wasn't afraid of hard work. I was young, healthy, and full of energy; I was ready to take on the world.

Farming is a rollercoaster ride. Like any profession, it has its ups and downs. I thought that I was "Living the Dream," but there were times when I had to question that assumption. Sure, I was my own boss, owned my own business, and I could take off anytime I wanted. Except that I didn't; I hadn't had a vacation in years. Wow! I realized that my business owned me, and I didn't even know it. I loved what I was doing, but I was getting older, and farming was getting harder. It wasn't as much fun as it used to be. The decisions were getting more complicated—payroll, insurance, and on and on. I had to continue to increase my farming operation to survive. It seemed never ending, and it was becoming more demanding, while profits were getting smaller.

But I was always looking for more income through new ideas. So, when my friend invited me to take a look at an idea that she was excited about, I thought I was too busy. I'd seen those things before. They don't work, and I didn't want to sell products. I almost didn't go along to find out more, but I am so glad that I did because I was pleasantly surprised. I saw a way to save a lot of money and create a really good residual income with the help of a team. I knew about teamwork. I had been on many teams during my lifetime, and I knew that a team could accomplish more than one individual. The residual income really got my attention. I saw a way to cut back on my farming operation and supplement my retirement. Now my dreams were beginning to change. The idea of "Living the Dream" began to take on a whole new meaning.

Warren Buffet says, "If you don't find a way to make money while you sleep, you will work until you die."

Do you want to work until you die? Do you want to do what you are doing now for the rest of your life? What's going to change in the next year, the next five years, ten years, or twenty years? Are you dreaming? Sometimes your dreams change. In my case, my first dream was to be debt-free and have enough money to buy anything I wanted. I accomplished that. But I had to put in sixty, seventy, eighty hours a week to have that lifestyle. Because of that, I missed so much time with my kids growing up. I was time broke. I had created a monster that I couldn't get away from. Farming was taking all my time. I had been taught to work hard, do your best, and you will make it. That's what we are taught in school. That's what society teaches us, the forty, forty, forty plan: Work forty hours a week, for forty years, and retire on forty percent of the income you were making. But that's not enough to live on. Besides, during those forty years, you are helping build someone else's DREAM! Why not start building your own DREAM?

I am writing this during the COVID-19 pandemic. Many people have been laid off or lost their jobs. A second stream of income would have made it much easier for them to deal with the situation. Money is not everything, but it sure does take the rough edges off.

"Dreams don't work unless you do!"

Most of us start with big dreams, then life happens. We go to work, help build someone else's dream, come home, eat, and go to bed. We get stuck in an endless, repeating cycle. Over time, our dreams begin to fade away and get crushed by life. Then there are the others who tell us that we're crazy for having a dream, saying, "You can't do that!" They don't dream, and they don't want you to dream either. NOTE: DON'T LISTEN TO THEM! They don't pay your bills. A wise man once said, "Sometimes the things we regret most in life are the risks that we never took."

What does "Living the Dream" mean? Is it possible? I believe that network marketing is the vehicle to accomplishing your dreams.

When I was first introduced to network marketing, I was working sixty to eighty hours a week. I had no time to spare. But, you know, we make time for what we want to do, and for what is important. I looked at several network marketing opportunities, but none of them seemed to be the right fit. I didn't really want to sell products. So, when my friend asked us to look at something that she was excited about, my wife and I were a little reluctant. But along we went, and we were really surprised at what we found. This time, it seemed to be the right fit and the right timing for us. NOTE: Find something that you love doing, and you won't work another day in your life.

Here's what happened to me: I had "Lived the Dream," but it had faded away until I was no longer dreaming, but I didn't even notice; I was consumed with farming. I was caught up in the rat race of life. Realizing this, I was open to looking at a new opportunity, and what I saw was a way to change my life for the better. This network marketing idea was exciting, and I began to dream again. For the first time in years, I was excited. I saw and talked to regular people who had transformed their lives from a mundane lifestyle to an exciting adventure. I knew that that was what I wanted.

It started with a thought; "If they can do it, I can do it." The wheels in my mind began to spin, and I couldn't sleep for a week. Everything starts in the mind, with belief. If you can see it and you believe it, you can achieve it. The mind is a powerful thing: You become what you think about. I began to think positively. I learned about personal growth, which I had never heard of before. I started reading books like *Think and Grow Rich*, *The Magic of Thinking Big*, and *Rich Dad Poor Dad*. I started watching videos of successful people. Personal growth has helped me in every area of life. I was so excited that I was going to sign up everyone I knew. Surely, they would be as excited as I was? But that wasn't how it happened, and I started to get knocked down. How many times do you keep getting back up? One more time? I love the great outdoors and like to deer hunt. I learned it from sitting patiently in the tree stand in the darkest hour just before dawn. The Bible talks about a time for everything, but it doesn't mention anything about a time to quit. Don't quit! Take it from one of the greatest basketball players of all time: "I missed more than 9000 shots in my career. I've lost almost 300 games. Twenty-six times I've been trusted to take the game-winning shot and missed. I've failed over and over again in my life. And that is why I succeeded."—Michael Jordan.

With the help of others, you can get back up. You can succeed. Don't quit until the miracle happens.

FINAL THOUGHTS

There's never a wrong time to start dreaming. Go for it!
Be open to new ideas. There's one that is right for you!
Nothing happens until someone gets excited. Be Excited! Be all in!
Do you want to change your life and your family's life for the better? Do you want to leave a positive legacy that will last for years after you are gone? If you do, you will have to take some risks. Remember, I mentioned earlier, "Often, the things that we regret most in life are the risks we were never willing to take."
Let me leave you with this thought:

Life is short, so don't let the sun go down on you before you "LIVE YOUR DREAM."

To God, Be the Glory, for with Him, all things are possible.

BIOGRAPHY

Richard Denning was born and raised on a farm in middle Tennessee, the home of country music, and has over forty years of farming experience. He loves to hunt, fish, play sports, and be in the great outdoors. He became a full-time farmer right after high school, helping feed the world. Over the years, he has also created an outstanding hunting business, Meadow Brook Game Farm, where he has met people from all over the world. Creating multiple streams of income has been instrumental in being a successful farmer. Richard has a passion for helping others. In this book, he talks about *Living the Dream* and how his farming experience has helped him successfully launch his network marketing business and allowed him the opportunity to show others how to create an extra stream of residual income.

Contact Information
Facebook: https://www.facebook.com/richard.denning.716

CHAPTER 22

THE ULTIMATE SUCCESS FORMULA

By Romacio Fulcher

In "The Ultimate Success Formula," my goal is to provide you with something simple yet profound that will help you in every area of your life, be it spirituality, finances, relationships, health, or your community. I will give you access to a formula that has never failed to work for me, no matter the situation.

I graduated from high school with a 2.5 GPA. I dropped out of college after 1.5 years, so I can tell you firsthand that I'm not the sharpest tool in the shed. In my 42 years on earth, the one thing I can tell you is that I'm really good at keeping things stupidly simple. The world we live in today is so complicated. There is so much going on that it is easy to feel as if you are drowning, lost, or confused. My aim today is to share a simple formula with you that is sure to work in every area of your life. I am excited to impart this to you, but I do ask one thing in return—when you read this, I want you to apply it instantly and be blessed because of it.

Let us talk about my Ultimate Success Formula. The definition of success, according to the dictionary, is the progressive realization of a worthwhile goal or worthy ideal. This means that the key to being successful is always to be sure that you are making progress. The reason why many of us become trapped and entangled in frustration in certain areas of life is that we are just not making progress. This is why I am confident my formula will change everything for you. It is truly a game-changer.

Are you ready?
Let us begin.

The first thing about the success formula is that it is critically important that you know your ultimate outcome. Consider your health, for example. If your goal is to lose weight, you must be clear as to exactly how much weight you want to lose—this is your outcome. Your outcome must be crystal clear. It cannot be blurry. Clarity is power.

If your goal is to make money, you must be specific as to exactly how much money you would like to make—this is your outcome. Your target must be precise.

If your goal is to find a mate, you must decide upon your preferences. Consider the personality traits of the person you would feel comfortable dating or marrying—this is your outcome. This is important because if you don't know your outcome, you may be tempted to settle for anyone. Remember—clarity is power; you must know your outcome to be successful. There are no exceptions to this rule.

Whether your goal is about family, relationships, or money, you have to know your outcome, and specifically what you want.

The second thing is to take massive steps towards achieving your outcome. This is the fun part. Notice how I did not say to take baby steps—I meant to take massive steps. If your outcome is to go from earning $20,000 to $100,000 a year in income, you must initiate a massive amount of action towards achieving your goal, according to my formula. This is important—you must take massive action. The more action you take towards achieving your goal, the sooner you will achieve the goal. This is critically important for you to understand. When you take massive action, you reach your goal much faster because you put more energy and effort into it. This applies to everything.

I took massive action when dating as a young man. You can probably imagine what that means. You will never be ashamed if you take massive action instead of taking just a little bit of action. Not only does this formula work in every area in your life, but it works every single time. All you need is the courage to take massive action towards achieving what you want. If you want something to happen right away, you have to be courageous and take massive action.

Number three is to always have a coach. What this means is that when you have a goal in mind, you should find someone who has already accomplished that goal. Let me explain why having a coach is important. Every single one of us has said, "I wish I had known then what I know now," at least once in our lives. You have probably also heard that hindsight is 20/20. With experience comes wisdom. Wisdom comes from banging your head against the wall as you make mistake after mistake until you eventually figure the problem out and become wiser. It also comes from learning from someone else's mistakes. This means that when you are trying to accomplish any goal, it is always wiser for you to learn how to achieve it from a coach who has already accomplished what you are trying to do.

I have a coach in every area of my life. Be it spiritual, health, money-making, or saving and investing, I have a mentor no matter what I do in life because time is the only thing in life that you cannot get back. You can make money and lose money, you can lose weight and gain weight, but the one thing you can't get back is time, so you must value your time, and to do that, it is smarter and wiser if you always have a coach.

Consider business, for a second, and the goal of making more money for what you're doing. Find a good coach. This does not ring true only for business. It can be for any area in life including spirituality, relationships, and health. To find a good coach, go online and look up the type of coach for which you are looking. Make a note of the top ten or 20 in the field, and find out who they are—this is secret number one. Secret number two is to find out how to get in contact with prospective coaches. When you do, ask them a single question: what do I have to do to make it worth your while to coach me on what I want to know? These two simple steps are how you can attract any kind of coach you want.

The question from secret number two is powerful because when you find the coach, you're not asking him/her to give you something for nothing. You are telling the coach that you are willing to work for what they know, exchanging your work for his/her knowledge. It shows the coach that you don't want something for nothing, which is very attractive to a coach and says a lot about you. Once again, it's really simple to find a coach. Look them up online—the top 10 or 20 in that profession. Number two, get a hold of them and ask them what it is that you would have to do to make it worth their while for them to teach you what they know. This is step number three. Always, always, always have a coach.

Finally, step number four of the ultimate success formula: gauge your approach. Let's say you have the first three right—if step number four is not working, then change your approach. You need to have an acute sense to know if your actions are bringing you closer to what you want, and if things are not working for you.

Now that you have the four steps of the Ultimate Success formula, I want to share all of the areas of my life in which I use this formula to be successful. This is the most important formula of my entire life, so let us take a look.

In the area of health and fitness, I have used this formula, knowing my outcome. For example, right now, I am in the process of losing 23 pounds in 30 days. I am 223 pounds right now, and I want to be 200 pounds within 30 days—I know my outcome.

Step 2: I'm taking massive action toward my goal. What does that mean? As an example, I prepare the meals that I eat every day. I work out with a trainer using a specific type of workout that will help me to reach my goal.

Step three is critical: I have a coach. As an example, I am learning from someone who has already lost 25 pounds in 30 days, and I am doing exactly what he did. I am eating the same foods and doing the same workouts.

Finally, step four—let us just say if I am 25 days into the program and I am eating right, and I am working out, but I am not making any progress towards my goal of losing 23 pounds in 30 days. That is when I would change my approach, according to step four.

I use this formula in every area of my life.

Let us talk about making money.

Years ago, in December of 2016, I was actually broke. I had made some very poor choices with my money and found myself in a position where I was broke. I believe that if something is broken, you should fix it, and I used the formula once again.

I knew my outcome: to save $1,000,000 over 12 months—not make $1,000,000 but save $1,000,000 over 12 months.

Step one: I knew my outcome.

Step two: I took massive action. I got involved with a business, and I went to work like you would not believe. I worked harder in that business in the first 30 days than I have ever worked in my life.

Step three: I made sure I had a coach, someone who has already achieved this goal before, and I made sure I did exactly what they told me to do.

Step four: if I had not seen progress by following the formula, I would have changed my approach. I continually gauged my results to see if I was getting closer to my outcome. Guess what? It worked!

On December 1, 2016, I was broke, and by December 7, of 2017, not only had I made millions of dollars, but I had saved over $1,000,000 liquid in my personal bank account for the very first time in my life, and I did it over 12 months. I made copies of it, had it framed, and posted it all over my house. My point is that it works in every area of life.

Let me end by asking you this: how many chances do you give a newborn baby to walk? The answer is: as many times as it takes. Some babies walk in ten months, and some of them walk much later in life, but by the time that baby is seven-years-old, all babies walk. This is why I say to gauge your results. If something is not working, change your approach and gauge your results. If it is still not working, change your approach again and gauge your results. If it is still not working, change your approach and gauge your results. These four steps will work in every area of your life. They are very simple—extremely simple! Do it now, and I promise you that your life will instantly improve.

I'm Romacio Fulcher, The California Kid.

BIOGRAPHY

Romacio Fulcher is a well-respected international leader, trainer, coach, and much sought-after mentor. He is a highly successful entrepreneur. He tried the traditional college path and quickly found that it wasn't for him. Instead, he began as a cold caller, getting leads for a mortgage company. Under the owner's mentorship, he mastered the business, ultimately going on to start his own mortgage and real estate company to become a self-made millionaire by the age of 25. He was introduced to his MLM mentor and the industry of network marketing about ten years ago. He applied what he learned once again to become a top leader and earner. Although Romacio has earned millions of dollars, his heart is in training and inspiring others to transform their lives by helping others earn supplemental income along the way.

Contact Information
Facebook: https://www.facebook.com/romacio.fulcher
Instagram: https://www.instagram.com/romaciofulcher/
YouTube: https://www.youtube.com/channel/UC1zB-1jmoOpJE_hg_aEPNZQ

CHAPTER 23

SHADES OF GREY

By Samantha Jung-Fielding

"For someone so intelligent, what on earth was I thinking? How did it get to this?" These thoughts tumbled around my mind as I gingerly touched my scalp, feeling the coin-sized bald patches where my hair was ripped out.

Something did not add up. Why did I stay in an abusive relationship with a man who tried to murder me four times? How much more would it take for me to wake up and smell the coffee? As things turned out, only one single well-aimed punch, not leveled at me this time. Instead, he hit the dog. He struck so hard I heard its skull crack. At that precise moment, I finally understood that unless I acted quickly, one of us would die.

It was January 1996, and I was 28 years old. One week after that incident, I ran away taking only the clothes on my back. I drove out of Belgium and down into France, heading for the ferry back to the UK. At a safe distance, I phoned him. His voice raged down the line, irrational, coercive, and demanding: "Did you take the TV? When I get hold of you, I'm going to rearrange your face. You'd better get yourself home right now and sort this out."

Although I initially felt I had the upper hand, over the next nine months, I desperately wanted to go back every single day. It was impossible to make a simple decision on my own. The psychologist outlined how the abuser and I had become co-dependent.

I was floored. Me? Co-dependent? What do you mean? My mother has dependency issues. Not me! I'm Miss Independent, the most reliable one. I'm the person the family depends on to hide family secrets, and being the eldest child, I was there to always save the day.

Except I didn't save this day. And now, locked in with my abuser, I had to find the key.

So, how did it get to this? What exactly had I been thinking? I was the first person in my family to go to university, yet how useful is intelligence if you still make stupid life decisions?

It was a revelation when I discovered how the mind works. Simply put, it's a game of two halves— the conscious and the unconscious! Everybody instantly relates to the conscious mind because its job is to think and reflect, to make logical and rational decisions. In university, my conscious mind was continually stimulated, daily contemplating new ideas. This is why the conscious is also called the thinking mind.

However, did you know the conscious only represents about 10% of the mind's total capacity? The remaining 90% lies in the unconscious, whose main function is storage and processing. The unconscious is responsible for automatic body functions (like your heart beating, digesting food, and correctly positioning your limbs for sitting, walking, or even climbing the stairs). The unconscious carefully files everything you ever learned or experienced, plus it stores your values, beliefs, emotions, coping mechanisms, routines, and habits. The unconscious is also known as the feeling mind.

In this marriage of the minds, it's critical to note your unconscious is operational from the moment of conception, while your conscious mind first awakens around your 7th birthday.

As a result, during the formative years, small children absorb everything without question. Their surroundings are readily accepted as a baseline or "normal" reference point, and they are heavily influenced by the people around them. In short, without any filters, they act like sponges.

This is all the more alarming when you realize your early patterns set a foundation for the rest of your life. This means your brain was programmed by a toddler, who mostly copied examples handed on by past generations (i.e., your parents, or even older!). Of course, you had no idea things could happen any other way. So, when the controls were passed to you, you left everything in place, permitting those automatic and established patterns to run their natural course.

And the fly in the ointment? Unproductive historical family blueprints. This explains why in January 1996, I was repeating patterns from my mother's personal history. It's unlikely to surprise you that my mum also survived an abusive relationship, including a murder attempt when I was seven years old.

To recap, intelligence (or lack of it) was not a factor in my abuse. Nor did it matter what I had been consciously thinking. Because I was unconsciously following a pattern learned literally at my mother's knee. And, it got to this because I had not yet learned how to break this unproductive cycle.

Shocking! Unfortunately, the implied consequence was even more severe. Unless I acted quickly, I would subject my unborn children to the same fate.

So, where to next? Brazenly attempting to avoid my mother's alcohol dependency, I had already shifted from being independent to co-dependent. Moreover, it's not like she never warned against the pitfalls of extremity. As a child, I repeatedly heard: "You're so black and white. What about some shades of grey?"

Was I to infer grey is the color of inter-dependence? The very definition of black and white (or polar opposites) is that neither exists without its opposite. There cannot be yes without no, day without night, or up without down. Perhaps the crux of extremity is inter-dependence, and any spotlight must shine on the continuum between?

Unfortunately, I was stuck in extremity. Looking back, I noticed I was always out on a limb. Mum named my brothers in honor of their uncles. Yet, I was called Samantha—after the witch on television. In 1964, Elizabeth Montgomery took the lead role in Bewitched. A twitch of her nose launched a fashion for naming daughters, which reached me in 1967. Years later, I discovered the origin of my name is Aramaic, and it means "the listener."

I grew up believing I was magical with the unshakeable conviction I was put on this earth for remarkable feats. My formative years provided few examples,

Aristotle's wisdom set my course: "We are what we repeatedly do. Excellence, then, is not an act, but a habit."

According to Dictionary.com, "A habit is an acquired behavior pattern regularly followed until it has become almost involuntary." John Dryden said, "We first make our habits, and then our habits make us." Experience had already shown me that habits run the show, but I was also painfully aware of what goes on behind the scenes. Emotions (especially negative ones) muddy the waters.

My mum demonstrated how those with unresolved negative emotions (like anger, sadness, fear, hurt, or guilt) tend towards the systematic repetition of problematic behavior. Consider the use of stimulants (e.g., cigarettes, alcohol, coffee, sugar, recreational drugs), binge eating, video games, road rage, cyclical/abusive relationships, overthinking and procrastination. What mum didn't know was that getting rid of the underlying emotion can be enough to morph a behavioral issue into a productive pattern.

Emotional release is an immensely powerful and transforming process, which unhooks the negative feelings from past memories. This allows you to remember an event or person without re-experiencing the sensations that were previously associated with it. For years I blamed my mother for ruining my childhood with her drinking. By taking full responsibility for my own future and releasing this extreme perspective of my past, I chose to feel compassion for Mum. In doing so, I paved the way for a positive connection with my own daughter.

In his book "The Power of Habit," Charles Duhigg highlights how every habit is unconsciously designed to produce an emotional reward. Realistically-speaking, any effective and long-term behavior change must, therefore, begin with emotional release.

Unpicking enough formative patterns creates a wide, open space to accommodate your most eagerly anticipated emotional reward. When I abruptly quit my second marriage, nobody understood my choice. However, I was aware my carefully crafted happiness was lopsided, and I was gifted a moment of clarity. Propping it up further was establishing yet another dysfunctional dependency.

I have long cherished the idea of two equal and opposite people coming together to develop a wonderful continuum (or legacy) of well-rounded children. Over the years, I was gifted with three magnificent boys. I always dreamed of having a daughter, but becoming a single parent at 41 shattered this lingering hope.

Since marrying my third husband, I repeatedly joke that on good days we are equal, but on bad days we are very opposite. However, it was no joke when I fell pregnant just two weeks into our relationship. True to form, Mum was less than encouraging when I announced the news: "Oh God! Not another one!"

In authentic witch tradition, my daughter showed up 13 days late. Having already waited 19 years for this child, a few more nights of sleep were neither here nor there. Her entrance into this world was bold and breath-taking. She birthed unexpectedly at home, with a theatrical fall into the toilet.

I already knew her name would be Maya, after my mother's mother. Imagine my surprise when someone later told me Maya means "mother" in the Tupi language.

A few months before Maya turned 3, our family emigrated from the UK to New Zealand. Known to the children as "Yorkshire Nan," my mum was heartbroken. She was sure she would never see me again. Barely a year later, she had a stroke which left her paralyzed down the left side. Some months after, I flew back to the UK to surprise her for her 70th birthday. That was the last time she saw me. After that, she slowly deteriorated and passed away shortly before Maya turned 7.

While mum waited for her curtain to fall, I rang her daily. She could no longer speak, so the nurse held the receiver to her ear and told me Mum smiled all the way through our calls. I chose to remain in New Zealand for the funeral, and my best friend from childhood attended on my behalf. There is a significant time zone difference, so I had just jumped into the car with Maya when I saw a phone message flash up from my friend containing pictures of my mother's wake.

Apparently, "A Whiter Shade of Pale" was at the top of the charts when I was born, and Mum had requested this song be played at her funeral. Without warning, the first melancholy notes drifted from the car radio as I swiped through the photos on my phone. Unexpectedly, Mum's coffin flashed onto my screen, and I began bawling. From the seat behind, a small arm crept around my neck as my daughter asked: "What is it? Is it your mum? It's OK, mama. Just remember when you were a little girl with Yorkshire Nan."

Maya's simple words of comfort contained wisdom beyond her years. Deepak Chopra says that to break through ancestral bonds that inhibit your ability to create the life you deserve, you have to understand where they originate.

No doubt you know someone who has spent a lifetime seeking. Yet, the answer is right there before you. Your family blueprint is already cast in black and white. It's the shades of grey that seek your attention.

I implore you to tread with compassion as you release negative emotions and unpick your formative programming. Your very existence is a formidable gift. Take the opportunity to design your unique pattern of productive cycles and happiness habits.

And be mindful that your children will copy your examples (good and bad!). So, I strongly suggest weaving slings and arrows of outrageous fortune through your shades of grey. Therein lies real magic!

BIOGRAPHY

Samantha Jung-Fielding is an award-winning speaker, author, and performance specialist in the field of habit formation and behavior change. Master hypnotherapist, master NLP practitioner, and certified business mentor, Samantha believes unconscious brain and body patterns hold the ultimate secret to your success. Corporate burnout led Samantha to establish a charity, co-found a business networking organization, and develop a radio chat show. She also launched diverse businesses, initially in traditional fields before expanding into network marketing to deepen her reach. When her family immigrated to New Zealand in 2012, Samantha and her husband opted to raise their children on a small alpaca farm in South Auckland. Had they understood the alpaca predilection for mischief, they might have thought twice about this choice.

Contact Information
Facebook: https://www.facebook.com/samjungf
Instagram: https://www.instagram.com/sam_jungf/
Website: http://www.happinessence.co.nz

CHAPTER 24

THE IMMACULATE JOURNEY OF A FAITHFUL WARRIOR

By Serah W. Muiruri

As I walk on my journey, my view of the world is one comprised of many dots, intrinsically connected and unique in their formation, the world would be incomplete if these dots were not strategically positioned to complete the whole. I am amazed at the purpose of each dot, each of them leading to my final destination; without any of these dots, that destination would not be as intended. Often, the purpose of the dot is not revealed on the surface, and if it is, its significance does not fall into place until the end approaches. As I toy with these thoughts, I realize that life is an entity forever unfolding, one that is full of contrast, complexity, uncertainty, confusion, mystery, and above all, vulnerability. These attributes continuously shape who we are day by day, season by season, and year by year. It is a maze that never ends, from its inception and our grand entrance into the world until the time we take our last breaths at the end of our incredible journeys and onto the next one, a rebirth into that unknown world we get to experience beyond our time here, on earth. We are, for today. When our mission is accomplished, we are gone, a little while later. During it all, the world continues to evolve in ways unimaginable. Our world is quite different from that of our ancestors. What determines our existence? Our core beings? Our essences? Is this the philosophical dilemma of nature or nurture? I can't help but think that how we end is shaped by who we are as unique beings, our genetic composition, our upbringing, our cultural backgrounds, our spirituality, our metamorphoses based on our individual experiences, and above all, the choices we make along the way. These choices are critical in crafting the masterpiece of our valuable selves. When these choices are in-line with our core values, we are more fulfilled, and consequently, a healthy equilibrium is born.

As I compile these words, my desire is to speak to someone out there who is struggling on her journey in a world that is often quite unforgiving and let her know that the world can and is still a beautiful place, in spite of the dark clouds. No matter what you face at the moment, the sunrise is always visible on the horizon. My mission and ultimate desire is to spread hope to the hopeless, to plant a seed of joy in those at their lowest point in life, and to let those in despair know that it is in those desperate moments that a new "us" comes to be. Greatness is derived from atrocities. These critical moments propel us toward something more significant, that promises a greater tomorrow. If we allow ourselves to have that experience, it will prove better than the day before.

Here's an extract from a blog post I wrote on March 12, 2014, titled "Uncovering Our Hidden Treasures – Our Childhood Dreams."

All of us had childhood dreams. At some point, we all wondered what we were going to be when we grew up. Then, we woke up one morning to discover that our childhood dreams and hidden treasures had been lost along the way. How did we get here so fast? Where did the time go? All of us inevitably get caught in the proverbial rat race, speeding through life, entangled in our desire to sustain ourselves. Then, slowly but surely, time creeps away only to discover that our childhood dreams have been forever shattered. Our childhood dreams reflect the joys of yesterday and our hopes for the future. We should all protect these dreams, feed them, and encourage them to grow. We must take care of our dreams, for someday they may take care of us.

I believe we are all destined to craft our paths as we nurture our unique individualities, which only we can define. This uniqueness is what separates us from others. Our goal in life should be to walk along this path without losing sight of who we are as individuals. It is critical to adopt a mindset that allows us to live lives of purpose, no matter the situation. We are drawn to be clinicians in the human services field because we want to give back to society, be it giving time or talent, always guided by the philosophy that we are our brothers' keepers. We are great at serving others, but it is easy to get lost doing the very thing we love the most. As my brother's keeper, I challenge everyone to do a little soul searching this season—take a brisk walk, feed the birds, listen to your favorite music, do some gardening, or share a cup of coffee, tea, or a meal with a friend you haven't seen in years. Do whatever appeals to you. Let us revisit our childhood dreams to renew them. They say that it is in the giving that we receive, but to receive, we must learn how to give to ourselves first so we can give more to others. We have all been given what we need; it is time to rediscover our purposes in life, which will ultimately help to shape our destinies.

Let's dig up our hidden treasures and childhood dreams.

Blog Reflection:

I wrote this blog about five years ago upon my CEO's request, which was based on taking a reflective journey through my life. At that moment, I realized there were common themes in my life that were instrumental in shaping me into who and what I am today. My being is a product of many things, and most are referenced in my abstract. Vulnerability has been a constant in my life as far back as I can remember. I joined the Mary Leakey Girls School for my A-levels in 1988 at the age of 17. I was only going to spend two years at the boarding school before I hoped to enroll in a local University in Nairobi, Kenya, upon graduation. It was the very first time I would be leaving the nuclear family of my parents and siblings. I was young, meek, lonely, shy, and unsure. I was consumed by these feelings as a youngster, at it eventually had an impact on my academics. Back in the day, Kenya only had four fully-fledged universities, and only the cream of the crop could attend these institutions. I certainly knew I had the brains, but my struggles hindered my desire to be the best I could. I barely survived, made few friends, and basically became a lost introvert in the large crowd. My only goal was to get through those two years, and I would be miraculously fine.

Two years later, I was back in the village, having been left behind while my colleagues headed to those higher institutions. How could someone like me, someone who was "First Division" material, be in this vulnerable position. I was 19 before I realized I needed to gather the courage to face the world head-on. A spark of hope was born within me, which was ultimately a defining moment. I will be forever grateful to my parents and the rest of my family for believing in me and instilling the value of hope, which would be incredibly useful in my journey of self-discovery. I would soon become a high school teacher—a good milestone—and that was only the beginning. After a long struggle and many challenges, my parents found a way to send me to the US for further studies. That was the turning point in embarking on my journey of discovery.

It was a hot summer's day in August 1992 when I left Kenya for the US. It was my first time on a plane, and it was a long flight. I landed in Boston, MA, with mixed emotions. As I navigated my way in that foreign land, I realized that my life was bigger than me, and my experiences at MLGS had not only prepared me for good grades but something bigger. These experiences gave me the tools and ammunition I needed to succeed in the US in the absence of family ties, and with only a few friends with the same life experience as me. From that point on, I knew I needed to craft my life not only to realize my dreams but to help others realize theirs as well, my family included. As the firstborn in an African family, it was expected that I would share the responsibility of helping raise my siblings, but now that I was in the "land of milk and honey," my responsibilities extended to those in my community.

Expanding Responsibilities

As a Catholic girl who almost joined a convent, the life I have lived has been in-line with what I perceive to be my purpose. My faith in God has been instrumental in this, and without it, I fully acknowledge that I would not be who I am today. Being the first one in my family to travel abroad—and nearly the first young woman from my village (in rural Ngarariga, Limuru, Kenya) to leave Kenya to further her studies—I became a key player in assisting families with young adults interested in joining me in the US. It was a task I executed willingly, as it is what I was destined to do. Yes, I made many sacrifices along the way. Often, I could not see how I could continue, given that I was earning meager wages and attending college while assisting others do the same. My parents could not pay for tuition fees because it was an impossible undertaking, coupled with the fact that I was perceived to be a responsible adult at that point.

To remain purposeful became my goal, and I focused on it. Today, my actions have had a positive impact on many families. By allowing myself to be a selfless instrument of giving, dreams were born, and they continue to be fulfilled. Most of all, my siblings were able to add to my pool of successful stories, and I now have the joy of being a part of their successes, as well as that of the others who have crossed my path over the years. In doing this, I gained much more than I would have, had I focused solely on myself.

Marriage and divorce were important milestones in my life, and perhaps the very best example of life's complexities and conflicts. Of all of the vulnerabilities I have experienced, these are significant reference points for me. I was married in a happy ceremony on a lovely fall day on November 13, 1999, to a gentleman I thought was my best friend. We had, after all, been everything to each other for several years prior to the big day, and everything was just great. As fate would have it, my marriage crumbled ten years later. To say I was devastated would be an understatement, especially considering the added tragedies associated with the painful break-up. How could the thing I thought the most natural be that complicated? As a childless African woman, the thought of being divorced was beyond painful. How did I end up here? How or where did I go wrong? What did I have to show for it? Why me? These and endless other questions rang like annoying bells in my head, and a daily constant for many years following. My divorce was downright nasty, and the experience was unbearable, ranging from domestic violence, immigration threats, societal biases, and invasion of privacy, culminating with video from cameras placed in my dwelling and vehicles. I was followed and monitored every step of the way, making fear my sad reality. My soon-to-be-ex accused me of poisoning him when his health suffered a downturn. It was a baseless accusation, with no scientific evidence to back it up, a ridiculous allegation. The status of his health only served to prolong my agony, as I was forced to halt divorce proceedings until he got better. It was a hurtful, grossly painful, and trying time.

My world had changed, and now, my community doubted me. My only true confidants were immediate family members and a handful of close friends who numbered no more than three people at that point. I struggled to pick up the pieces, knowing I had no other choice. My faith in God kept me going, magnifying my resilience to greater heights. Amidst all of this, I focused on my job and caregiving responsibilities for "my Jen." Her being in my life gave me a sense of value and a higher purpose, keeping me grounded and focused. My coworkers at the time were a great source of support as well, and I remain forever indebted to all of them. It was at this lowest point in my life that I discovered an appreciation of and beauty in being alone as a journey of self-discovery. For the first time, I was able to distinguish between loneliness and being alone. My inner-strength was amplified; it was, indeed, the time for rebirth. Jen remains my purpose today, as do all of my nieces and nephews, who also give me a sense of validation. Nathan and Nayva have been especially instrumental in my healing process. I now know, for a fact, that my life is still unfolding. My parents, siblings, George, Martin, Grace, and Damaris, as well as my extended family, have continued to believe in me even when my strength appears shaken. I know my well-being matters to them, and particularly to my parents, who are aging gracefully.

Letting go of the bitterness was another facet allowing me to enjoy life after divorce as it was meant to be. It was not a simple decision; it was, however, necessary for me to move forward. Trusting that this milestone was part of my ongoing journey, I accepted the situation as it was. Thus far, I have gone through a restoration period, and by God's Grace, my success story is still unfolding. I know all too well that in faith, my destiny is well-crafted and spectacularly designed.

As a life coach, I understand that operating from a judgment-free zone is a happy place to be. Allowing myself to view others through their own lenses was another instrumental discovery. Most of the time, people do the best they can with the resources—which are often limited—they have; perfection is but a myth.

The lessons I learned:

- always allow yourself to be vulnerable, as it is in this state that optimal growth is attained
- humility is a virtue of honor—strive to be humble at all costs

- everyone crossing your path is there to fulfill a purpose, good, bad, or indifferent
- embarking on a journey of self-discovery when surrounded by adversity sets a beautiful stage for living a more fulfilled life, which often leads to the healing process
- nothing great comes easy, and if it does, the fruits are only short-lived
- always allow yourself to be an instrument of peace, regardless of the atrocities around you
- stay focused on your quest while searching for your true purpose in life—this revelation will save you in hard times and will provide a great reference point as you navigate through your day to day challenges
- once you find your purpose, strive to execute it at an optimal level
- become that which you were destined to be
- remain true to yourself and others; allow yourself to remain authentic to your values
- aim to have a positive influence on others, but do so with a sense of humility; expect nothing in return
- the good you do will always come back to you ten-fold
- where there is a will, there is always a way—just DO IT
- your inner-strength is greater than you realize—it is insurmountable
- the choices you make will have long-standing effects; choose wisely
- if you deviate from your intended path, forgive yourself and get back on track—nothing remains constant
- appreciate those around you
- have faith in a higher power (God for me)—this deity will always be a part of you and guide you through life
- spend time connecting to your inner-spirit—this regular check-in will speak to you in a gentle voice that sounds loud to your inner ear.

CONCLUSION

Trust that your journey will unfold and end the way it was meant to. Always guard your spirit and keep your head high, even when you have no clue what the next minute will bring. Seize the little moments in life, for they are gifts that continue to give. Your preparedness will influence your ability to receive the seeds that will grow into sweet fruit. Amidst this dance of life, we are but unique *dots* that make the world complete.

BIOGRAPHY

Serah Muiruri is currently licensed as a certified rehabilitation counselor serving as a master level clinician in the ever-progressive field of human services. Serah works for Nonotuck Resource Associates Inc., a local agency in the state of Massachusetts. Serah's career began in the early 90s after emigrating from Kenya, her country of origin, to the US. In her tenure of service, she has held several positions, serving children and adults with disabilities and often multiple diagnoses, including Autism Spectrum Disorders, intellectual and cognitive challenges, and acquired brain and trauma injury, among others. Her intrinsic drive to see others succeed has influenced Serah's attraction to the field of network marketing, and she has successfully created sizable networks. Additionally, Serah is a trained life coach, specializing in neurolinguistics.

Contact Information
Facebook: https://www.facebook.com/serah.muiruri

CHAPTER 25

RESCUE MISSION

By Sheen Marshall

I was on the last of my three jobs for the day. Driving around gives you plenty of time to think about yourself, your situation, and life in general. The previous two days, I had driven for twenty-seven out of the last thirty-two hours. It was brutal and dangerous because I was so tired that I was drifting while driving. I wasn't doing it because I had a love for driving. I was doing it to help make ends meet for my family.

During those long hours behind the wheel, the same thought kept going through my head: "What am I doing wrong?" Crying out to the Lord, as I have done countless times, I couldn't stop asking myself what exactly was I doing wrong that my life would have gotten to this? Life was nowhere near what I had envisioned it would be as a forty-year-old. My family was struggling financially, and we were just barely making ends meet. Our home was in foreclosure, and the business that I launched a few years prior was failing with $85k spent and not a single penny back. It was a terrible situation to be in, and one that I wouldn't want anybody to have to go through. I kept asking myself how a person with a B.S. and Master's Degree could find themselves living this way. Hadn't I done everything I was supposed to? I had followed the system of going to school, getting good grades, and getting a job. But this had led me to being forced to drive twenty-seven out of thirty-two hours just to earn enough money to, hopefully, cover the basic bills. There was that question again: What am I doing wrong?

Sometimes when you're drowning, the Lord will send you a life raft. It's incredible how often I see the life raft thrown to people and they push it away—and continue drowning. I refused to allow my story to end like that. I never wanted any handouts or freebies; I just wanted a shot. I needed the fire to burn inside me again. I needed to be reborn and to dream again. I needed hope. Fortunately, all of that happened for me in December of 2016. That was the day that an old friend that I hadn't seen in ten years flew into town, without telling me that he was coming, to throw me a life raft. Often, though, we will block or ignore a blessing because it's not wrapped up in the package that we want it to be or expect. So many of us become lost, meaning that we wander through life without a purpose. We haven't found the reason why we are here. I have been fortunate enough to find my purpose, and I'd like to go back a bit now to share with you how I discovered it.

As I look back to those grueling years of driving around as a delivery driver, getting no sleep for little to no money, I always knew that there was something bigger for me out there. I knew that this wasn't my final pit stop. I was still holding out hope that my failed business, a fantasy sports website, would take off, but the grim reality was setting in. I wondered if it was time to finally give up on that dream. But then what? That was the big question. I was previously a teacher for fourteen years, and I was certain that the profession was NOT for me. I disliked it so much that I let my teaching certificate expire because I didn't want it to be an option to fall back on. Leaving that profession, along with starting a business, led me to become a delivery driver for multiple companies. I remember showing up for work daily at one of my driving gigs and looking around at the others doing the same thing and wondering how we had all ended up there. There was a man formerly successful in banking, an armed forces veteran, a man who had a successful business and was now in his late seventies, as well as many others, including myself, and we were all forced to deliver delayed luggage for little to no money (that was one of my three delivery jobs). I kept wondering what mistakes we had made in life to end up having to do that for a living.

I used to be one of those people who believed that very successful people were always cheating or had some unfair edge over everyone else. Although this may be true SOME of the time, the fact is that very successful people spend lots of time working on themselves. How do they do this? It's called personal development. Amazingly, it's not taught in schools or society in general, NEARLY as much as it should be. When my old friend flew into town to throw me a life raft, what he did was introduce me to personal development. This was through the company I joined, which he was already a part of, that is BIG on personal development. As I started getting deeper into personal development and learning more, it was like an awakening took place within me. I started learning things about myself and others.

What's one of the biggest ways to work on personal development? By reading books, which was one of my BIGGEST weaknesses in life. I never liked to read books. Prior to February of 2020, I hadn't read a book in over fifteen years. As a man with two degrees, it was shameful to admit it. I have heard a saying in the past three years that goes, "success leaves clues."

As I started to observe and follow the people that had the life I wanted, I noticed that a common thing amongst them was the fact that they not only immersed themselves in personal development, but they also read books religiously. While I was sitting stagnant in my company and failing to advance in rank, I began to notice that, often, when someone was being interviewed, at the end of the interview they would be asked, "So what book(s) are you currently reading that you could recommend?" Person after person would quickly be able to call out a book on personal development that they were reading. And I sat there thinking to myself that I was going to beat the system and not follow the playbook by not doing any reading. Meanwhile, I'm looking dumber and dumber.

One of the crucial turning points for me was when I was fortunate enough to be invited to spend the day at the house of the founder of the company that I'm part of. It was on this day that I TRULY learned how much I DIDN'T know. The bible says, "My people are destroyed for lack of knowledge," and if that ain't the truth, then I don't know what is. The founder of my company talked to a group of us for six hours straight with no break. No matter WHAT the question or topic was, he pulled out a book and was able to flip to a page to answer or address it.

For six hours straight he did this, while I was sitting there saying to myself, "How stupid can you really be to think that the people who have the lives that you envy all read books constantly, but you think you're going to be the one that makes it to where they are without reading at all"? It was at that moment that I realized that my purpose in life was starting to take shape in a manner that I could only have dreamt about.

One of my favorite hip hop artists of all time is a rapper called The Game. He recently released his tenth studio album, which is titled *Born 2 Rap*. He was asked in an interview to explain the title of the album. His answer to the question has resonated so deeply with me that I recite it often. He said that (paraphrasing), "Everybody is born with a purpose. You don't know the point in your life that you are going to figure that out or when your purpose is going to find you." It took YEARS of struggling, headaches, sadness, and trials for me to find my purpose because it damn sure wasn't wrapped up in the package that I had expected it to be.

Nevertheless, I found it and embraced it. I was fortunate enough to discover my purpose in life and my destiny. The reason why this chapter is called "Rescue Mission" is because I must go back and rescue my people. When I say, "my people," I'm not just referring to the black community.

"My people" refers to all those who have realized that they weren't put on this earth to struggle to live paycheck to paycheck, be born and die in generational poverty, and not to advance personally or professionally. I believe that God didn't put us here to struggle. For so many, the daily struggle has become as routine as brushing your teeth and tying your shoes. My mission is to take all that I have learned on my personal development journey and use it to help those who haven't learned or been taught these things.

My people are crying out for help, and I am here for them. My mission is to show them that all of their dreams and desires can be attained by investing in themselves. You have LOTS of fight left in you to be the person that God has called you to be, but you must stay in the fight until you realize who you are and are willing to develop and grow into that person. Maybe you are someone who has yet to find their purpose in life? If that's you, then I say to you Godspeed because the journey will be WELL WORTH IT. Just keep fighting and it will happen. If you are reading this and have determined that your purpose is to rescue others as well, then our Rescue Mission has just begun, and I look forward to going into the trenches with you to help and save as many as we can.

BIOGRAPHY

Sheen Marshall is a network marketer who spent fourteen years as a school teacher. His career in network marketing has allowed him to help others find success in the industry and has also led him to discover his purpose, which is to help those who truly want to live and not just be alive. His passions include traveling, exercising, sports (especially fantasy sports), reading books, and listening to audios on personal development. He is also an active member of Omega Psi Phi Fraternity, Inc.

Contact Information
Facebook: https://www.facebook.com/rausheen.marshall
Instagram: https://www.instagram.com/big.sheen05/

CHAPTER 26

WHAT MOST PEOPLE DON'T UNDERSTAND ABOUT NETWORK MARKETING

By Steinar Pettersen

It's now more than two decades since I first became involved in network marketing. The first company that I was introduced to was selling a health product, and after attending the first meeting, I felt very excited about my prospects. I remember talking to my mother about it back then and telling her the things the company had told me during the meeting. It's so easy, I said, the product sells itself, and I'll earn a lot of money. However, I saw myself quitting my job after a couple of weeks because I thought the marketing opportunity would be such an easy and lucrative ride.

Readers who have worked in network marketing will recognize the kind of lies companies feed you when they're trying to enroll you—which I fell for—and the damage done by this sort of misrepresentation is something the network marketing industry must take responsibility for. It's the reason why many marketers all over the world have been overselling in a way that has ultimately harmed the whole industry and given it a bad reputation. The result is that new and innocent marketers struggle at the start of their careers.

During our discussion about the new role, my mum asked me straight out, "Who do you think is going to buy all these products you are selling?" "You are!" I said. "No, I'm not," she replied. She'd already noticed that the product had quite a small target market, and thought it was unlikely to have a mass appeal.

Looking back, I realized that my mum had already figured out the catch, but I had to figure it out the hard way.

Fueled by courage and enthusiasm, I felt I was moving forward, always looking for my next target, even though I hadn't enrolled in the company. Despite that, I was dedicated.

Around this time, a friend and his wife came to visit us at our home. I was excited as I started to tell our guests about the company and the product, and how I was expecting to make BIG money with almost no effort. But my friend interrupted me, saying, "Steinar, I've already enrolled with the company you're talking about." Surprised, I asked him how it was going. He told me that he had so far failed to enroll anybody or shift any product at all, despite having a basement full of products that he'd paid for. His wife suggested that he try to sell some of it, but he said she could have a go at doing it because he didn't want to. We all had a good laugh about that.

That proved to be a fateful conversation for me, and you could say that my good friend "saved" me from network marketing at that time. After learning about his experience, it dawned on me that this was far from an easy way to make lots of money with little effort. I think it's because of the way that the idea is sold to many freshly recruited marketers, as it was to me, that most of them don't understand why they end up struggling with their business and lose money. They're given an unrealistic idea of what's involved and think they've joined a network where they don't have to do anything but watch the money come rolling in. But guess what? Network marketing is hard work, like any other business. If you want to succeed in your career, you have to put in the hours.

Looking back, I think I have always been a dedicated guy, someone who easily gets excited about new things. I remember getting my first real permanent job at sixteen while I was still studying to become a mechanic. I vividly recall the day I drove out to the farm on my moped and applied for the job in person. It involved taking care of the animals, feeding them, gathering eggs, and milking the cows during the weekends and vacations. I was thrilled when I got the job and felt so proud when I was able to tell my parents. It was through that job that I learned to take responsibility at an early age. At that time, I was so dedicated to agriculture that I thought I was going to be a farmer. However, after finishing studying mechanics three years later, I already knew that the one thing I wasn't going to be was a farmer.

So, I got a job as a mechanic, working with pressured systems: first steam boilers, and then pressure air systems. Because I'm from Norway and come from the area known as the country's "Oil Capital," I had the opportunity to work offshore in the North Sea on oil installations as a technician on the air and firefighting systems. I had other missions, too, working as a course instructor when our company oversaw the gas contingency onboard. In total, I worked offshore for around fifteen years, an experience I value very highly. Then, about ten years ago, I moved into the sales department of the company. I had a flying start and made a new record for sales. Everything was good, and everybody was happy.

However, a few years later, there was a crisis in the oil industry, and everything came to a halt. Sales levels dropped dramatically, and my boss changed the rules about sales payments. Under the new regime, all sales personnel would only be paid for the sales they closed during personal sales meetings and not when orders came *through the house*. As I was selling the most expensive products, I was the biggest loser in the new system. I was unable to make anywhere near the same level of sales through meetings as before, so my income fell sharply, and before long, I found myself frozen out of the company.

You can imagine how my self-esteem plummeted. I was at rock-bottom. It was then that I decided to leave sales for good and never return. So, I got a job working as a technical manager in one of the biggest greenhouses in Norway.

Six months later, in January 2017, my upline Frank gave me a call out of the blue. He asked me if I would like to come to a meeting the following Sunday. I said I would if I didn't have to sell anything, and he assured me that it was just an opportunity that he wanted to offer me. So, I went along to the meeting and sat through the presentation. It all sounded so good that I got super-excited again, and agreed to sign on as a customer, although, in my heart, I really wanted to sign up as a marketer, as well. However, I remained somewhat skeptical, as I'd lost some money on other scams previously.

Consequently, I told Frank that I needed some time to consider signing up as a marketer but would stay in touch. I hit on the idea of enlisting some of my friends to join me at the next meeting, thinking that I'd wait to see their reaction; if they joined, so would I. If they didn't, then neither would I. I felt that this would act as a sort of insurance. But I made a big mistake; I revealed to my friends what the meeting was about.

In Norway, network marketing has a terrible reputation, and most people don't want to get involved. Norway is one of the wealthiest countries in the world, so people usually don't have to take a job if they don't want to. There's a welfare safety net for the unemployed, although it certainly won't make anyone wealthy. However, right now, like most people, I'm not sure how long this safety net will last after the coronavirus pandemic. I've heard people in Norway saying on the news that they've only got a few kroner in their bank accounts because the new payment system designed by the government to support people during the pandemic isn't yet working as planned.

Anyway, after I told my friends what the meeting was about, they bailed out, and I did the same. Some days later, my upline called me again and said that he'd heard that the meeting was canceled. I confirmed that it was and told him that I was still skeptical. But Frank didn't take no for an answer, saying that he was sure I'd regret it if I didn't enroll. I didn't like what he said but ended up enrolling anyway, and also enrolled one of my friends who was willing to take a chance.

Once I'd enrolled and started working, my old dedication for network marketing returned, and I found that I really liked the new company. Nevertheless, I remember finding many excuses not to pick up the phone and start recruiting new people. At the time, I didn't have the right skills to do it successfully.

It's worth mentioning here that, in my experience, this is also something people starting out don't fully understand about network marketing—to do the work successfully, you need the proper training and the tools.

I soon started to join new meetings and began taking part in training sessions. I remember we had a visit from one of the company presidents during a meeting. He asked the room, who was willing to leave their comfort zone. I was the first to raise my hand, and he asked me to come up on the stage. I remember him telling me about some of the events that were planned. It was profoundly exciting, but he didn't understand why I thought all this was such a big deal.

Not long after that, I attended my first event in Torino, Italy. It was a fantastic experience, with a far bigger crowd in attendance than I had ever imagined possible. Eric Worre was conducting the training, and I could relate to everything he said. As Eric was lifting us all up with his step training, I was so fired up that I dared myself into doing something I would never usually do. During a break in the training session, I was chatting to a musician from a band that I like, when Worre started walking through the audience. I thought to myself, if he passes me, I'm going to give him a handshake. And that's precisely what happened. Later, Frank said that I was the only person who had successfully managed to divert Eric from his usual routine at such events.

I must say that it was at this training event that I think Eric Worre changed my life. I really want to thank you for that, Eric!

After the event, my career suddenly kickstarted—I went from Level 2 to Level 5 within a month. I remember being so full of energy that I sometimes had to let off steam by screaming in my car as I was driving along. Seeing my success, the company invited me to a leadership conference in Vienna, where I met the founder of the company.

My motivation to work was at its peak, plus I had great mentors who helped me get better at the job. We all put a lot of time into it. That reminds me to thank my lovely wife, Siv, who patiently put up with me spending so much time on developing the business. From time to time, she joked that the new business was my new wife.

Even when Siv and I were on a holiday in Spain, Eric Worre was with me on the sunbed, not physically, but in my ear and on the screen. I was learning how to recruit twenty people in thirty days. While I was training, I also started to figure out how I could put my own twist on the job. I began preparing for presentations, calling my father from Spain, and instructing him how to do a drawing for me that would make it easier to get my message across to people at meetings. By the end of the holiday, I had completed the training, which was like getting a monkey off my back. I found I was genuinely enjoying the business and having fun.

Many people don't understand that an important aspect of network marketing is the support you get from others. Plus, you can start your own business from home, and no formal educational qualifications are needed if you're willing to work hard. As I see it, one of the biggest problems facing the industry is that many people aren't ready for that level of responsibility and hard work. Several factors can get in their way, and the biggest is the fear of rejection. Many starting out are simply not adequately prepared for this, so when the fifth person says no, they give up. There's an easy remedy to this problem: if uplines give newly enrolled people more time to do the training step-by-step, then I'm convinced that many more would succeed. It seems likely to me that, after the coronavirus is contained, people will be more receptive to the business and the network marketing concept.

Sadly, the network marketing business I worked for closed in Norway about two years ago. It gave a lot of people an excuse to quit. I didn't quit. Instead, I focused on getting more training. In fact, during the family's celebration of my mum's seventieth birthday in Italy, I was still doing live training courses with Frazer Brookes on my cell phone. Thanks, Frazer, for all the great training sessions, and the books!

I'd like to send a special thank you to Matt Morris, who has supported me daily with great emails, live training, and other videos. He's always happy and full of energy, and I want to thank him for all the times he's lifted me up when the going was tough, and I wasn't producing any results.

I'll sign off by saying, because of network marketing, I am now back in sales.

BIOGRAPHY

Steinar Pettersen comes from Sandnes in Norway. He is an entrepreneur and business coach. After starting out as a mechanical engineer working offshore in the North Sea for the oil industry, he has since enjoyed a long and successful career in network marketing. He has participated in many network marketing training events hosted by industry luminaries such as Eric Worre, Tony Robbins, Frazer Brookes, and Matt Morris. Steinar is also the founder of a video production company. He's now dedicated to helping people succeed in their network marketing business.

Contact Information
Facebook: https://www.facebook.com/steinar.pettersen.98
Instagram: https://www.instagram.com/steinarsin/
Website: https://www.futurehomeoffice.com/

CHAPTER 27

FROM GO TO WOE...
AND BACK AGAIN

By Stephen Davis

I was born at the bottom of the world with sixty-six million sheep and three million people, and pastures and scenery as far as the eye could see—my home, New Zealand.

A beautiful place and at the time when parents left their kids by themselves, cars were packed like sardines, and you left home without locking the doors... well, scratch that last bit, I grew up in one of the lowest economic places in New Zealand, and if you didn't lock the door, then you would probably lose that door among other things.

Devoid of any cell phones, internet, or video games—in fact, there was barely a TV with two channels—we made our own fun, created our own adventures.

My childhood was full of life and mischievousness. I belonged to a generation of kids who were left to their own devices for hours on end and, as you may imagine, did everything you can think of.

We turned the house into a bomb zone, the coffee table into a sled, we even practiced flying off the roof, jumping off rooftops and through windows of numerous houses, played tag around glass doors, somersaulted over concrete fences, let strange kids in our homes, lit matches, and firecrackers inside, made our neighborhood block into our "Olympics" park, turned our park trees into makeshift climbing walls, and crawled underground into partly-laid pipes by local authorities with nothing but a torch and courage.

I broke things, lost things, messed up things, climbed everything you can imagine while safeguarding my explorer spirit.

It was not surprising that I ended up with battle scars and in trouble several times. But I wouldn't trade it for anything, for it made my childhood memorable and led to an adventurous life.

I developed a knack for losing things. I lost my school term bus pass regularly and ended up running to and from school daily. I became extra fit, but it wasn't so great when the bus driver who often gave me free rides, asked my mother why I was running all the time? Ouch!

I was also "famous" for repeating the same mistakes. How many times I spent kneeling on the lounge floor with my siblings, saying sorry to mum and promising never to repeat the behavior, only to do it all over again the next week. The perils of such cyclic behavior came to haunt me later.

I harbored a few insecurities. Growing up with mixed heritage, I didn't fit into either culture and there was prejudice too. My parents constantly fought, and this meant that from as young as a preschooler, I was often the barrier between whether one got hurt or not.

We moved cities at a key time, which meant that I had to start new friendships and adapt while tackling the adolescent worries of pimples, hair growth, and low self-esteem issues.

In my new city, on New Zealand's beautiful South Island, my high school science teacher Mrs. Metcalfe, who upon seeing an insecure young man, said, "Stephen, you have a beautiful smile." To date, I am grateful to her for the positive reinforcement she gave me.

Sometimes the simplest comments can leave the most profound impact; positive or negative. Since then, most people often notice and compliment my smile.

Being "famous" as a child can be far more fun than painful. But as an adult, it entails entirely different things.

Remember when I said I was known to repeat the same mistakes?

I led my life by following meticulously carved plans. I was striving to fulfill my vision. I was married, owned a house, had a growing family, and a career to see me through to retirement. I had money saved and money growing, all was going according to the plan.

I was leading a life that most people dream of.

But as fate would have it, in a short amount of time, I lost it all. I came home from work one day to find the house half-empty; my wife of ten years was gone with the kids. I was forced to sell the house and watched half a million dollars disappear down the drain. With my career finished, my reputation hit rock bottom. Some "friends" and "loved ones" turned a blind eye while muttering "God bless," "All the best," etc.

I felt that the Universe was out to get me and I crumbled under surmounting pressure. Blaming God, the Universe, everyone, and everything else, I retreated deep into my shell. My health plunged, my hair greyed, my weight ballooned, and for the first time in my adult life, the future looked bleak.

The pain was so great, the depression and numbness so debilitating that I struggled to even leave my parents' home, which I had returned to for some respite.

I was barely alive, let alone doing anything else. My life had fallen apart dramatically.

But, lost in the middle of this perfect storm, I found a way through. And no matter what you encounter, I assure you there will always be a way through for you too.

Here's what I discovered, and may it help you in your time of need and guide you toward the life that you seek.

Key 1: Take Time Before You Are Forced to Take the Time

I remember the night that was the culmination of everything that occurred. I had no home, not even my parents'. Out under the stars at the beach, I contemplated my life and the possible future that lay ahead of me.

I had not pondered so deep in decades or asked any existential questions. It's no wonder I was a mess.

It is better to take a deep, hard look at your life before you have no other choice than to do so.

Key 2: Reach Out; Save Yourself Unnecessary Pain

At times, a third person and their objective perspective could become a key difference between a life mended or one torn asunder.

Before I slept, I phoned some people who played heartfelt roles in my life, and in doing so, it stopped me from doing anything stupid; stupidity which would have further derailed my life.

Key 3: You Can Change

Being on my own, with nothing, going nowhere, I had plenty of time to think. During that time, I had a deep realization.

It didn't matter wrong had been done to me, and how bad the situation is, it did not have to dictate the rest of my life. I could change it; the power was in my hands.

The realization freed me, and I began to let go. I was free to rebuild anew.

For the first time in ever so long, I slept peacefully.

Key 4: Look and Listen Carefully for Life's Clues; Learn early, Save Pain Later

Life has a way of sorting us all out—call it God, a higher power, or the Universe.

I started recognizing patterns in my life; different people, places, and times but repeated situations, with an almost déjà vu precision.

I thought, "How could this keep happening?" "What was the connection?"

I then had an epiphany—these were situations that I hadn't learned from, situations I had not resolved properly. It hit me like a ton of bricks.

In hindsight, I could see that throughout my life, I was "famous" for repeating the same pattern of dealing with situations. Consequently, I hit the same insurmountable walls over and over again.

It was clear how each similar situation became increasingly worse, leading up to the hardest time in my life.

I created a recipe for disaster by putting a band-aid on deep wounds and carrying on, until my life fell apart.

Key 5: Your Life Is 100 Percent Your Responsibility

I gained a new perspective and was shaken out of a victim mentality— "Why me?" or "How unfair!" Instead, I replaced it with a new understanding that my life was my own responsibility, no one else's. Soon, the questions changed to, "Why not me?" or "Life can be unfair, so what?"

It was the kick in the proverbial backside I needed, and I was so grateful to finally learn the lesson.

You can let life do you in, or you can take life and make it happen for you.

Key 6: Clear the Rubble of Your Life

It's one thing to get through something, it's a whole another to get over it. Throughout my life, I recall many situations where I held grudges for such long times. It was during the hardest time of my life that I felt the full weight of holding onto those grudges. I could feel the pull of those grudges dragging me down.

I lived for two years in such a damaged way that it compelled me to think of the finiteness of life. I came out, and adopted the motto, "One life, live it fully, have no regrets."

I properly processed what happened, felt the pain, forgave, let go, and moved on. Notice how I didn't say hide or forget the pain. If you try and do this, the pain has a nasty habit of resurfacing again, in unattractive ways, and at embarrassing moments.

I decided never would I let any situation ever cause me to dwell on it so long again and I haven't.

Ask yourself would you rather spend fifty years or more getting over something, blaming others, and being right . . . or let it go and live your best life?

Time does not care if you mope around for five minutes or fifty years. It ticks on, indifferently.

Now unless you know that you have an extra life or two up your sleeve . . . save yourself unnecessary life-sapping energy.

Key 7: Step Forward, Do Something Constructive with Your Life

From the worst soil grew a bud of hope. Within a week, I had a roof over my head, my kids with me, and shortly after, my new employment secured. I then began to rebuild the shambles of my life with a new foundation.

I took counseling, gained inspiration online and offline, and connected with people globally. I watched, listened, learned and grew, spent time discovering who I was, and doing things I loved.

A lifetime of developing an unhealthy mindset takes some time to dismantle.

I did not shy away from asking difficult questions to myself and others, for I knew it was needed to overcome the hurdles of a regressive mindset. Find your inner child and be courageous to give new things a go. In doing so, you will stretch yourself, grow, and discover the whole new *you*.

Remember, no will always remain a no if you choose to do nothing. So ask, do, and give yourself a chance of being the best *you*.

FINAL THOUGHTS

Why do some harvest their true potential, find success, and be financially well off, while many others continue to struggle? It's the barrier in their mind that gets in the way.

So . . .
Key 1 - *Take time before you are forced to take the time*
Key 2 - *Reach out; save yourself unnecessary pain*
Key 3 - *You can change*
Key 4 - *Look and listen carefully for life's clues; learn early, save pain later*
Key 5 - *Life is 100 percent your responsibility*
Key 6 - *Clear the rubble of your life*
Key 7 - *Step forward, do something constructive with your life*

Be that person who considers things most won't, take action where most don't. . . and you'll gain the life that most miss out on.

And Where Am I Now?

Healthy, fit, in a loving relationship, a great dad with wonderful kids, an author, a successful businessman, and moving quickly toward fulfilling my lifetime vision of being a global mentor, trainer, and inspiration.

Like nothing will stop me, let nothing stop you.

Break preconceived ideas, notions, and a lifetime mindset. Let go of pain and the things of the past.

Remove the barriers, build afresh, and abundant success will follow.

BIOGRAPHY

Stephen Davis is a mentor, coach, and successful networker. He is passionate about helping others to succeed, inspire, and impact their lives. He works out of his home in the beautiful garden city of Christchurch, New Zealand. He likes spending his summers camping and adventuring locally and abroad with his darling and their four children. If you look closely, you might find him dancing among the treetops . . . but not too closely, he has already fallen once and broken both wrists.

Contact Information
Facebook: https://www.facebook.com/StephenJDavisOne/
Instagram: https://www.instagram.com/2dreambelievelive/

CHAPTER 28

JUST DECIDE - THERE IS NO OTHER OPTION

By Steve Eastin

What happens when you finally decide that failure and living an average life is not an option?

What's holding you back?

Is it your age? That's only a number.

Your ego? Do you think that you can do it on your own?

Your choices? Okay, maybe you haven't made the best of choices, but you have to let that go.

Your past? Let it go.

Your mistakes? We all make them; just let them go.

Your financial situation? There are a lot of ways to make money—take a risk once in a while.

The negative people around you? Find new people.

Your own negative thoughts? Start creating positive ones.

The haters? This is my favorite one—prove them wrong.

Easier said than done, right?

My journey to mastering the above started when I was 11 years old. My mom and dad were entrepreneurs at heart, and they worked extremely hard. I watched them go to work, buy an apartment complex, create businesses, and build relationships.

Around the 11th year of my life, my dad made a statement that has stuck with me ever since: "You will never get rich working for someone else." This indicates that proverbial turning point (a noun referring to a decisive change in situation, especially one with beneficial results).

Dad led by example; his actions said what words could not. In the book *Rich Dad Poor Dad* by Robert T. Kiyosaki, the Rich Dad describes my father to a T, but I did not read that book until later in life. It wasn't until reading the book and taking stock of what I know now that I realized that my dad and mom were actually mentors and teachers.

Dad and mom eventually fired their bosses and continued with their investments and businesses. They were true entrepreneurs. Unfortunately, my dad died in his semi-retirement at the age of 44 in a small plane crash in Alaska while enjoying a hunting expedition. I was 19 at the time. Dad was on his way to millionaire status, but Death and Destiny had different plans for him.

After watching my parents when I was 11-years-old, I decided to get a jump on things and start my own lawn mowing service. I made some contacts, lined up some customers, and away I went. The money was good until the weather turned cold. The money after that came in the form of payment for household chores. It was not as good, but there was still money coming in. I always had multiple jobs throughout high school, but nothing significant.

When I hit 20-years-old, a new turning point occurred when I married my high school sweetheart. I convinced her that I would give her everything she desired because I would be a millionaire by my 44th birthday. I promised that our lives would be remarkable, worthy of attention. Unfortunately, I never achieved my goal. My theory is that I started to work for other people, helping to make their dreams come true instead of my own.

I worked in a mailroom and as a bartender. I still mowed lawns, and I was a cashier at Target. There were also some purifier sales and a job as a sales representative later in life. This pattern continued, allowing me to support my wife and enjoy the birth of our daughter. We lived in luxury—kidding! It was a two-bedroom apartment where the cockroaches were so big that we named them and called them our pets. Through it all, I knew that if I kept working at these jobs, it would soon pay off.

I worked my way up from that mailroom to customer support; at least I was moving up. It still felt as if something was missing. I knew that I was not answering my calling, nor was I keeping the promise I had made to my wife. I had this burning desire to help people and be in a position of authority, so I quit pretty much all of the jobs I had, including the customer service position. Next, I decided to be a police officer at the age of 30—it was always something I had wanted to do.

Supporting two children now, I graduated from the police academy—from which, I might add, several people were pretty surprised that I had (take that, haters). I first became a reserve officer, then a paid dispatcher, and I was eventually sworn into the patrol division. Trust me—I could write an entire book on that 18-year tour of duty, but I'll save that for another day. I will, however, tell you that it changed my life.

Believe it or not, my pattern of multiple jobs continued during my police career. While working as an officer, I started a trucking company, a construction company, and a trailer refurbishing company, all of which were operating at the same time at one point. I managed employees, did the accounting, spent time at the various locations, swung a hammer—you name it, I did it all while performing my police duties to a high standard. I never slept, but by God, I was going to be a millionaire by the age of 44. My future was bright. The money was pouring in.

All was good until the economy crashed. I will spare you the details, but shit just happened. I lost everything in a blink of an eye: savings accounts, toys, businesses, and the house. And then the ultimate happened: bankruptcy.

If you have ever experienced the feeling of not knowing where you and your family are going to live after you have uprooted them from everything they knew, it cannot be explained, but it sucked!

We lost the home on our 60 acres, but we were blessed to find a townhome in our community that served its purpose over the next few years.

During that time, I chose not to quit but stayed more positive and more determined than ever to succeed.

The bankruptcy taught me that I was doing it all wrong. Though I was working extremely hard, I had decided to assume the responsibility and blame for my situation.

I truly felt that God had put me in that position to let me know that striving to be a millionaire was about nothing but greed. And something was still missing, but I could not figure out what it was.

I got my real estate license in 2009 while still a police officer, continuing the pattern of working multiple jobs, and it has worked out well over time. I was back in the financial fight, but unbeknownst to me, I was still in the proverbial rat race.

These two professions began to take their toll on me, becoming more demanding and time-consuming. There was no such thing as sleep, family time, or vacations. Unfortunately, I became more selfish than before, which led to a downhill spiral for the worse. I started to become a recluse, I did not want to spend time with anybody, and I just stopped being me. I was not the kind of person others wanted to be around.

One day while on patrol, I received a text message from my daughter. In it, she laid out the truth. She advised me that I could do anything, that she and the rest of the family wanted me back, and that I should retire. This was interesting because I was the type of person that you could not tell what to do, nor would I take someone else's advice. It was a brave thing my daughter had done. Thank God, I listened to what she said. It struck my soul, and I knew she was right because I felt at peace.

Ironically, my commander called me into the office later that day to see what I had decided about my schedule for the following year. The schedule had been written on a whiteboard in his office. I found myself staring at it long enough that my commander asked me for my decision once more. I knew I had to save my relationship with my family, and I had to fix me. I looked at my commander and told him I was giving him a week's notice. He stated, "You're f****n kidding me!"

After we determined that I wasn't kidding, I agreed to a two-week stay to assist with training my replacement. After the two weeks, my agency gave me a fantastic retirement party, and I left law-enforcement. I am very grateful for my agency, and I would not change anything about my law enforcement career. I believe it was a journey that I needed to take.

To all of the family members of men and women in law-enforcement, the military, and first responders: thank you so much for what you do, I know what is involved, you are special, and I pray for all of you every day.

Holy crap! Now, what would I do with no job, very little savings, a small 401(k), and no real estate deal in sight? I guess you could say that I took a leap of faith.

I was pretty much in survival mode for the next year or so. My savings were not big, and the IRS loved me. I searched for my next turning point and what I had been missing.

The answer was simple: I just dropped the ego and asked for help. By that time, I had surrounded myself with some amazing mentors who gave me the advice to read books, take pride in myself, invest in some self-development classes, my mind, my financial education, and my training, so I did. What do you know? They were right. Most importantly, I devoted myself to God and stopped doubting him and the power of prayer.

I finally understand that you can't always do things on your own and it is okay to ask for help. I've learned about financial strategies and that relationships are more important than anything. It taught me how to create a focus board and values list and to visualize my goals and create affirmations. Trust me on this one: write it down, or it won't happen.

I now know my destiny, and I have found my core purpose in life. Life is no longer about my wants, needs, or material possessions. It is about the wants and needs of other people. It is about helping people to become leaders. It is about helping people succeed in helping others invest in themselves. It is about helping people to create a lifestyle of their own that they can control. The bottom line is, I needed to figure out how to become a leader for the right reasons before I could help others do the same.

To all who are reading this book, decide that failure and living an average life is not an option, and age is just a number. Start your positive transformation today. You can do it. I believe in you.

To my wife: I have not quite reached millionaire status yet, but thank you for being so remarkable and never giving up on me, no matter what.

BIOGRAPHY

Steve Eastin has been in the public eye for over 20 years. He has worked with thousands of people in different aspects of their lives and is deemed by friends as a successful life coach. His educational experience consists of ethics training, crisis intervention, crisis and business negotiations, and leadership and self-development. Steve is a successful entrepreneur with growing businesses. He is married to Brenda since 1986 and is blessed with a son, Danny, a daughter, Amanda, a son-in-law, Calvin, and granddaughter, Indiana Cree.

Contact Information
Facebook: https://www.facebook.com/profile.php?id=100009492462937

CHAPTER 29

PERCEPTION IS EVERYTHING

By Syen Yap

Have you ever wondered why some people seem to have so much good *luck* in their lives with everything always going their way? They just appear so positive and bad things never seem to happen to them.

I'm embarrassed to admit it, but sometimes I want to hate them, or at least feel green with jealousy. It's not fair, right? Well, it's always been a mystery to me, so I decided to try to discover if some people are just born lucky. And, maybe, along the way, I might figure out how to get luck on my side.

I came from a normal family with four siblings. However, my parents got divorced when I was in secondary school—when I was about fifteen years old. A lot of people might think that might not be a great situation, especially during our growing-up journey.

But today, I'm actually glad about that event; we children no longer had to keep listening to the arguments or endure the hostile atmosphere at home every day, when we came back from school. I now think it's good that both my parents took the next step, so that the changes allowed them to live much better lives.

Yes, it was challenging for me and my siblings when our parents separated. I followed my mom, and my siblings followed my dad. I took this path because

I felt that I understood why my mom made the hard decision, and I wanted to at least be by her side. My siblings and I communicated by letters, with me only going back once a week during the weekends to visit them.

There was one time when my youngest brother forgot to bring the house key, so, after he came back from school at around one in the afternoon, he had no choice (without a phone) but to sit by the front of the house, under the hot sun, waiting for another sibling with a key to arrive around seven in the evening. After a couple of hours, the next-door neighbour realized the situation and allowed him to wait inside their house, while he waited for the other sibling to return later that evening.

When I learned this, I felt so sad that my younger brother had to go through that. However, there wasn't a single time I blamed my parents or the divorce for it. I decided back then to always believe that things happen for a reason.

I am proud to say that, having gone through this life-test while growing up, all my siblings became very independent and mature compared to their friends of the same age. We rarely asked for help from a parent unless it was absolutely necessary. We monitored our own education, deciding on the courses we would take by ourselves. Even then, all of use understood that each person has to craft the life they want by themselves—that we are all responsible for our futures and no one else.

Fast forward to my life as an adult, and you might agree with me that my difficult growing-up journey had a purpose behind it. My attitude about life back then has now come full circle, and I still make decisions on the basis of my belief that our responsibility in life is to be the type of person that is a blessing to others.

My first job was in the hotel industry as a sales executive, followed by a second in the exhibition industry. Within these two entirely different environments, I was blessed to have a supervisor who really took care of me, always fighting for me, and earning my goodwill. I discovered that, as with growing up, there are workplace politics that threaten to drag us down. However, I instinctively chose not to participate in them, simply because such entanglements create so many problems—and there is never any gain.

Here are a few examples: Once, I shared this practice of positive perception with one of my colleagues, Joseph. I told him that I thought I must be a truly blessed person because I had so many great people around me. He replied, "That's because you always have an attitude that everyone appreciates—you always look at everything in such a positive way. So, all the negatives seem of such little importance that you cease to care about them."

Then, a year ago, I became involved in my first network marketing company. At that time, our team was not very strong. It seemed as though many people were thinking that they would wait until the team grew stronger or the brand become popular before they would commit to joining because they thought it would then be much easier for them.

But a voice inside whispered to me, "Why don't we become the *pioneers* and make it work when others won't? Isn't it challenges like this that create the greatest opportunities for us to learn and grow as people? The best memories we have in life are often of overcoming the challenges that, at the time, felt like the most difficult. But I say that those are the times when there is the greatest opportunity to build a strong foundation.

And, although our team was small, I'm so grateful that we had a great leader with the long-term vision of building something strong together. How grateful I am to be to be part of such a team!

Then, in early 2020, the COVID-19 pandemic arrived—the virus that took away thousands and thousands of human lives. People everywhere are suffering because of the coronavirus. Countries are in lock-down, with people asked by their leaders to stay at home. The world has been forced to freeze all economic, social, and physical development activities. Many people are genuinely worried whether this will be the end of the world, as the impact of the virus seems greater than any other event in human history. And it's happening globally. Will we survive? And if we survive, how will the world function in the future?

Yet, a few months on, the great news is that there are many signs that Mother Earth is healing herself. Plus, there are other positive outcomes—like the decrease of air pollution from factories and autos. We have better air quality. And not only that, but the quality of water has shown significant improvement in Venice, as well as in rivers in India. Wild animals have appeared in groups to reclaim their territory, and the Earth's ozone layer is healing by itself.

But does this remind us of how much damage we have done to our Mother Earth for the sake of so-called progress and economic gain? Can the pandemic be seen as a warning, a lesson from Mother Earth to force us to stop and think deeply about what we have done with her kindness? Have we wondered why COVID-19 has spread so quickly and lethally amongst humanity, forcing us to stay at home for the safety of ourselves and others, while the animal kingdom remains untouched? You could say that the animals are now claiming their "freedom" back from us.

Maybe we should be paying greater respect to Mother Nature? As humans, we claim to be the most intelligent among all the living species on our planet yet when we look at the bigger picture, we see that we only play a small role in the greater scheme of things.

Perhaps Mother Nature is reminding us to be more than just takers, selfishly squandering her bountiful resources? By focusing only on our personal gain, have we truly forgotten that we should also give back and show our care for her?

Today, I sit quietly in appreciation of the situation. This pandemic may be the biggest opportunity for humankind to grow and gain that it has ever had. It may be saving us from the day of reckoning that will come at the end of the world. I believe that, if we wake up and take better care our planet, we might save ourselves from utter extinction.

If I may, I would love to share with you an idea of mine that comes from the center of my soul; today, globally, I believe there are two types of people facing this pandemic:

Type 1 – Focusing on the virus, blaming others as to why it is happening, while the virus continues spreading due to the stress created by peoples' constant complaining.

Type 2 – Accept the situation and take it as a challenge, looking for a solution while feeling grateful for being safe and healthy.

Please don't misunderstand me—I'm not asking you to be oblivious to the fact that bad things happen in life. Of course, they do. And it's okay to acknowledge that we do not know how the future will turn out. But my life has taught me that what matters is how you choose to look at things: Do you perceive certain situations, like the pandemic, as "Bad Luck" or "A Great Challenge"?

I wish to share with you the secret that has helped me in my life: If we decide to take up the power residing within us that comes from choosing how we respond to life's challenges, that directly affects how we feel inside. Instead of choosing to be a victim, we can choose to live as great students, constantly pushing ourselves to rise above the expectations of our great Professor and earn the best grade we can. I believe that power lays in the way we look at any given situation and our mindset affects the consequences resulting from the actions we choose to take.

It begins with your choice of not *what* but *how* you choose to believe. It's all a matter of perception. For instance, I choose to believe that things happen for a reason, and that outcomes are a result of what we did or failed to do in the past. Think about it this way—that life may be testing you, giving you an opportunity to begin to transform yourself into who you're meant to be— a better version of yourself!

Yes, I could have chosen to blame my parents about not giving us the best lifestyle during my childhood. Yes, I could choose to complain about why my career path has had so many ups and downs and difficulties. Yes, I could choose to blame others for this pandemic. But there is something that I know within the depths of my soul: None of these behaviours will serve me well. None of these beliefs will change the situation for the better, and all such negative emotions only hurt me.

But if I *choose* to accept the situation, switching my way of thinking—my perception—gives me the *courage* to face all these wonderful challenges with positivity. Because, in my experience, challenges usually mean an opportunity to grow and become a better version of myself.

Remember, as human beings, we do not have the power to control what will happen. But we do have the power to choose how we respond to life's challenges by deliberately aiming our intent towards the outcomes that we want to achieve.

My friend, please be grateful for whatever happens in life. Every event is a meaningful piece in the grand puzzle of life, one that helps us paint the story of our lives that we can recall again and again when telling it to our great grandchildren. When we inspire them with our courage to make the best of life's challenges, we are seeding the power of positive perception into their minds and ensuring that their world will be even better than ours.

BIOGRAPHY

Syen Yap is a professional executive in the exhibition and network marketing industries. Challenging career environments have built her tough and resilient character that always looks for solutions to problems through a positive mindset. Her life experience and positive attitude in life has successfully helped her create an influencing power over more than one hundred people, who have been inspired to change their way of thinking. Syen loves adventure and enjoys outdoor sports, such as diving, riding, hiking, and camping. By the age of twenty-six, she had traveled to more than ten countries. Her passions include inspiring others to live with gratitude and living her life to the fullest by sharing her story and lifestyle.

Contact Information
Facebook: https://www.facebook.com/si.yen.14

CHAPTER 30

Pulling Your Own Weight

By Toni Catchings

I remember when I first started playing sports. All my grade school friends were playing soccer, so I wanted to play too. Soccer came easily to me, and I found that I loved the game. As I got older, I became interested in playing for a better team in a more competitive league. The team I was hoping to play with was highly successful. To join the new team, I had to try out. The coaches would have all the aspiring players perform the same tasks, and then they would pick the best performers. I remember watching a tryout so that I could figure out what was required. I realized that, to be successful, I needed to practice, practice, and practice again. My dad would go with me to a local football field and help me practice. Finally, the time for tryouts arrived, and I made the team. I continued to play with this team for the next five years.

The team coach was a little intense. He had really high expectations of his players. For instance, if your uniform shirt came untucked during a game and you didn't fix it immediately, he subbed you out of the game. Practices were always challenging. We started every practice with a one-and-a-half to two miles timed run. Then, we had to complete one hundred sit-ups, followed by jumping rope for a specific number of successful jumps. Once everyone had completed this, then practice began. At the end of practice, we always finished with both fifty and one hundred yard sprints. At this time in my life, I REALLY hated running. But I knew that if I wanted to play with this team, it was just something that I had to do, whether I liked it or not. I was learning how to carry my own weight, although I didn't even know it at the time. I did know that I was definitely part of a TEAM, and that we were working and playing for and with each other both on and off the field.

When I was nineteen, the team was invited to represent the United States in an invitational international soccer tournament in China. Back then, there were no U.S. women's national or Olympic soccer teams. We won most of our games, but we also had a tie with China and a loss to Australia. We still qualified for the semi-finals and made it through to the finals. But, of course, who did we have to play in the finals? Australia again! We had already lost to them once. Did we honestly think we could beat them?

I remember feeling super-nervous when the final game started. We made it to half-time, and the score was still tied nil-nil. I remember seeing my teammates do things that I had never seen them do before during that game. The determination that we had to come back and beat this team was INTENSE! Everyone on the team took care of business. When the final whistle blew, my teammates and I were exhausted by the supreme effort that we'd put into beating our opponents, but the feeling of accomplishment was overwhelming. Final score: USA one, Australia nil.

Now, as an adult, I realize that the coach pushed us so much to make sure that everyone could carry their own weight during a game. We would all be able to push through and continue to play until the whistle blew at the end of the game.

I have another soccer championship memory, where I did not carry my own weight. It was during another final game to determine the best team in the country for our age group. We were tied with the other team, and they had control of the ball. The next play involved the player I was responsible for marking. I remember thinking to myself that she would mess up, and I could relax a little. My poor decision to relax and not give it my full effort changed the game; she made the right play and did it well because I wasn't challenging her. I underestimated her will to win and her ability. Within the next few minutes, that team scored a goal.

I KNEW it was my fault. We never came back from that. The other team won the championship. I had failed my teammates and myself. I remember that poor decision to this day. My lack of effort let down eighteen other people and all our fans. Even now, years later, I often wish that I could go back in time and have that moment back—and make a different decision. Of course, that's impossible, and I must live with it.

Life continued, and I found myself divorced at the age of twenty-seven after five-and-a-half years of marriage. This utterly crushed me. I felt ashamed of the situation because I felt as though I had failed. I was not proud of having to admit that we could not work things out. Now, I had to figure out how to carry my own weight in my new single life. I needed to figure out how to remain living in my house and continue to make a car payment on a small salary. Honestly, I was really struggling with the divorce, both financially and emotionally. I had allowed myself to become emotionally dependent on my husband. Once again, not a proud moment.

I was suicidal during this time, thinking of more than one way to take my life. Of course, my parents and friends knew I wasn't myself, but I never told them about the negative feelings and thoughts going through my head. Then, a friend of mine invited me to join her husband and her at a church service. I went along and, after that, continued to participate in going to church. This was the step I needed to get past the divorce and move on. Allowing God back into my life was a game-changer. That was when I realized that I needed to start carrying my own weight again in my personal life. I made a decision: I needed a better paying job and to start taking care of myself again.

I had always wanted to help people by becoming a paramedic and ride an ambulance. My ex-husband had always discouraged it, but now I went for it. Within months, I applied for a position with the fire department to pursue my dream of being able to help others. I realized that I needed some serious training to prepare for the physical ability test. Once again, I found myself doing the hard work that was needed to be successful. I prepared by pushing (by myself) a full-size pick-up truck through a church parking lot numerous times a week. I also pulled tires loaded with bags of concrete through the park. I was determined to pass the test.

The day of the test arrived. I was extremely nervous but ready for the challenge. I remembered during the last section of the test that I needed to make an adjustment to the equipment, but the voice inside me was telling me, "Don't stop! Keep going, just do not stop!" I listened to that voice and completed the test with only one second left on the timer. The test wasn't perfect, but I was successful because I had prepared for the day.

Welcome to the Fire Department! Now I had to figure out what was required to carry my own weight daily in rookie school as a firefighter and as a paramedic. All rookies must prove themselves once they graduate and are assigned to a specific station. This is a situation where you have to pull your own weight, or you might as well go and find another job. Understandably so; firefighters have to go into burning buildings when everyone else is running out, and they may need to carry someone out. Even for the guys, proving yourself as a trustworthy member of the station crew is hard. But for a female, Holy Cow! Even the general public doesn't believe that a woman can be physically strong enough for this career. The answer to proving yourself is to take things one step at a time, and always give one hundred percent effort to every task. Even the menial tasks, like mopping the floor and cleaning the toilets, you must give it your all. When a fire call comes in, you must step up and be prepared to use everything that you were taught in rookie school. On the inside, your adrenaline is pumping like crazy, but on the outside, you appear calm and collected. You have to keep moving forward and taking one step at a time, even when fear is setting in.

Over the last twenty-seven years as a firefighter and paramedic, I have experienced a lot of different situations. I reflect on each one to determine whether I pulled my own weight. I always ask myself if I could have done anything differently to affect a different, better outcome? One specific incident that I vividly remember was when a thirty-year-old male was shot multiple times by teens who were just out shooting randomly at people for no reason. The fire engine arrived on the scene first, and the man was still talking and able to communicate. My partner and I arrived in the ambulance a couple of minutes later. Now, the guy was no longer talking. He was unconscious. We placed him in the ambulance and began taking care of him. But by the time we arrived at the hospital, he had deteriorated. We performed CPR but were not able to save him. The immediate feeling I had was that I had failed. I felt I had let the man and his family down. After all, I am supposed to be the angel that comes in and makes a positive difference.

This incident replayed in my mind for days. Every time I replayed it, I knew there was nothing else I could have done. Both my partner and I had pulled our own weight. We knew what to do, how to do it, and when to do it. We were prepared for the situation. We made all the right decisions and had both given one hundred percent effort to saving the man, but we still had no control over the final outcome.

Of course, it's at times like these when we have to accept that we're only human, there's only so much you can do in some situations, and despite doing your utmost, you're going to be unsuccessful at times. I have failed and am going to fail again at times, just as we all do. But can something truly be called a failure if I give one hundred percent of myself in the attempt? Yes, I may be unsuccessful, and I get very disappointed and unhappy when things don't work out the way I want, yet I find that it is easier to accept the outcome if I know I gave it my 100%.

Stuff happens to everyone. That's life. But you have to decide if you want to be an asset or a liability. You have to ask yourself if you're going to be crippled by what happens to you, or empowered by it. I choose to be empowered! I want to carry my own weight in life and continue to get up every day and improve on my life. I realize that the real struggle is within myself, as it is within all of us, and the real battlefield is in my own mind. To achieve what I want to achieve, I must relentlessly battle against the negative thoughts, the lack of energy, the bad days that come to us all. I understand that the decisions I make in my mind every day affect my everyday actions and outcomes. Do I go to the gym today? Or do I take it easy and chill? Do I practice today? Or do I decide that it will be okay if I don't prepare?

To me, it's an incontrovertible truth that we control our own destinies through the decisions, or lack of decisions, that we make numerous times a day. All of us know this, but often we still let life make the decisions for us, and we simply go along with them, even if they're not what we really want. I believe that we must do the opposite and make the decisions that determine our lives for ourselves. Are you happy to let circumstances control you? Or do you want to control the circumstances? Life seems to me like a chain of events requiring decisions in every corner, and a wrong decision or a failure to make a decision is like a weak link in that chain that can affect our whole lives.

I say, do not allow yourself to be caught up by circumstances—don't be that weak link. Instead, take some time to figure out what needs to change to make you a stronger link—and then take the appropriate action! Keep taking one step at a time and moving forward. Try to keep improving yourself, and always keep learning. It's up to us as individuals to decide what needs to happen to make sure that we pull our own weight in our lives.

BIOGRAPHY

Toni Catchings is best known for two things: Being a strong athletic woman and her compassion to help others. She was inducted into the Sports Hall of Fame at Texas A&M University-Commerce in September 2015. She continues to serve as a firefighter and paramedic. She has been promoted through the ranks over the last twenty-seven years and currently holds the rank of Captain. She enjoys helping young girls realize their true potential and to believe in themselves. Toni is also the owner of Catch 22 Home Solutions.

Contact Information
Facebook: http://facebook.com/toni.catchings.3
Instagram: https://www.instagram.com/monkee2022/

CHAPTER 31

CHOOSE MENTORS AND APPRECIATE FAILURES

By Tonika Bruce

I believe I was destined for greatness with a purpose to lead people. My greatest satisfaction has always come from helping people. I can look at a process and quickly suggest ways to improve it, and think of several related businesses, only to see that idea become a multi-million-dollar business within three or four years.

When 9/11 happened, I was 23-years-old. I thought it was the worst day of my life. My business seemed doomed. No one was buying or selling; people were too busy, in shock, glued to the TV. I went from making 30K a week to being afraid to buy a bag of ramen noodles. I lost everything—money, pride, and the fire within. I didn't know what to do. I had no real friends. I couldn't ask my family for help. How could I ask anyone who hadn't ever been in such a situation for help?

I credit this as my turning point—the moment when I realized that chasing money isn't the right way to do things.

I kept asking myself the same questions over and over: How did this happen to me when all I know is how to be successful? Do I see success only one way? In just one area of my life? With only certain people?

At that age, I didn't take the time to reflect on what had gone wrong; I was broke, hungry, and prideful. I thought God was angry with me. My best friend had committed suicide, and I knew how that affected me and everyone else, so that was NOT an option. It seemed as if my only choices were to hustle or just give up.

I graduated from college, enjoyed a successful career playing basketball, and was ready to continue living the so-called all-American dream. I reconnected with the love of my life, got a great, high-end apartment, and started working until the time was right to go back to school. But even with three jobs, money was tight.

Then, I saw an ad that said $20/hour: I called the number and got an interview. I arrived early and was immediately drawn to Alan, the presenter. Watching him completely changed my life. I was deeply impressed by the way he commanded the room and connected easily with the 50 people in the room. That day, I felt I'd seen what success looked like—wrapped in an expensive suit, with conviction in his voice, Alan had the ability to make people *feel* what he felt. I took the job and used my rent money to purchase the required kit. It was my first direct sales position; even with zero sales background, my competitiveness, my desire to be the best, and make a ton of money drove me from the start.

My biggest growth came from modeling Alan and reading several of the books he referenced.

Being naturally gifted and ambitious, I wanted to be the best; I advanced quickly and earned the opportunity to work with the owner of the company in Ft. Lauderdale. One of the most important lessons I learned is that having the wrong mentor can negatively influence your chances of success if you aren't strong enough to fight against their effects. After a few months of working in Ft. Lauderdale, I was ready to go out and open my own location in Dallas, TX. I prepared by attending events with people like Tony Robbins, Mark Cuban, Zig Ziglar, and Les Brown. I learned that everything was possible—when I took action.

My plan was to open 300 locations in 10 years. We opened eight offices in 6 months. I did interviews, hiring and training over 3000 sales representatives. At the young age of 23, I was easily making a six-figure income monthly. I studied, developing myself into a great speaker and teacher, even at events outside of my own company. And then, it happened: I didn't just fall, I plummeted and landed flat on my face.

After that day, I decided it would be best if I didn't try again. I was broke—I had maybe $50 at best, plus credit collectors were hounding me with daily calls. Never in my life had I ever felt so scared, hurt, or angry, and I had no idea of what to do to get out of the situation.

It wasn't long before that $50 became $10, which was when logic and necessity won out. I desperately needed money, so I got a job to fit in better with the people around me. First off, I tried restaurant management. True, the hours were long, and I smelled of cooking every day, but the money was great, and I soon became successful again. I even managed to grow our restaurant to new levels. My time in restaurant management taught me the value of giving good service, as well as humility, but soon it felt like it was the right time to leave the fajitas behind and try something closer to my heart.

That's when I first got into basketball coaching. I had the opportunity to watch the grind, hustle, and enthusiasm in my good friend, Dorian. He commanded attention, and his intensity was infectious. Before long, his positivity drew my thoughts back to the dreams I'd once had of greatness. My purpose and passion for leading, training, and developing people was leading me back to my roots, and my first passion—basketball. Being naturally competitive, I loved winning, so playing for championships was always top on my list of great ways to spend time. In a short period, I'd exchanged my expensive suit for gym shorts and sneakers. Okay, so the "vehicle" had changed, but so had the quality of the mentor. That, as I was to discover, was the missing piece of the puzzle.

There's no denying that I enjoyed incredible success as a basketball coach. But, although I coached a team that won five championships in a single season, it seemed as though the athletic director's sole mission in life was sabotaging my players and team—just because we were successful! It was this that helped me officially confirm my understanding of mentors and the influence they can have upon you. It made me realize how important it is in life to carefully choose the people and things you learn from. As I discovered, if you surround yourself with the wrong ones, your greatest accomplishments can be spoiled as a result.

It's sometimes hard to accept, I know, but trust me when I say that a bad mentor can come in many unexpected forms; it can be a boss, the company you work for, a friend, co-worker, or parent. At the time, I couldn't help wonder if I was the only one who had come across a boss or a group of people apparently dedicated to causing me to fail. I'd always believed that bosses, managers, and the people around you are supposed to be rooting for you and helping you to succeed. Clearly, I was wrong.

Then, without warning, things for me just seemed to hit a wall; I was at the top and climbing in my coaching career. I had over ten interviews and got seven job offers, just not the three I wanted. I felt like a failure again. I felt like I was deliberately being brought low, and this time I wasn't sure I had the will to get back up.

After my grandmother passed away, I was led into a completely new and different field—nursing. I had gone from sales, public speaking, coaching teenagers to wanting to care for geriatric and cardiac patients. But I wasn't sure that nursing was even worth getting excited about. Maybe this was God's way of saying that he wasn't mad at me anymore and that he was giving me another shot? One thing I was sure of, though—this was significant. It told me that my life meant something, and whomever I was becoming, it better be good! By this time, I'd witnessed first-hand the terrible standard of care that patients were receiving and wanted to remedy that by being the opposite—I wanted to be THE BEST!

Nursing school was absolutely exhausting! Anyone making it out alive has rightfully earned the title WARRIOR BEAST. The small town of El Dorado, Kansas, hosts a hidden gem, one of the best nursing schools on the planet. During this time, more than ever, my growth as a leader was challenged and elevated. Yes, there was a moment when I felt like quitting, when hearing the voice in my head of my high school coach, Coach P, saying, "Finish what you start and make things better than you found them," just wasn't enough. My turning point came in the third semester, when I came across an instructor named Sherry. Sherry was super tough, which made me want to be in her clinical class. Not only was Sherry tough, but she also demanded a lot more from her students than other instructors. Under Sherry's teaching and mentorship, my previous expectations of what was "standard" shot up the scale. She made me see that what I'd been giving and contributing so far was simply not good enough.

In nursing school, I became president of my class for two consecutive terms in a row and formed lasting friendships with several classmates and instructors. I was honored to be the commencement speaker at our graduation ceremony. This re-ignited my fire for public speaking and encouraged me to study for my master's degree in Executive Leadership.

My quest to give my patients the best care possible was often clouded and compromised by a lack of resources, insufficient staff, and lack of teamwork. I took a job to be a part of something great and believed so deeply in the hiring manager's vision that I was willing to drive 90 minutes each day to reach the goal I had in mind. I wanted to be a part of that success, but when both my managers left, my motivation changed, and I found myself once again no longer positioned for success.

Arriving at a place where success was truly represented in the people around me, and finding a suitable mentor were now the most important things to me. I wanted to experience success, not just read about it on a vision board, so I continued to search for my "fit." My purpose changed from wanting to lead people to searching for a leader to lead me in the right direction.

The day finally came when I decided that I was going to be the best leader I knew and that, to achieve that goal, I had to make myself better. By chance, I crossed paths with one of the most influential leaders and mentors I have ever come across in nursing—my then Chief Nursing Officer, Molly. Molly's motto was, "make it happen." Her smile made her look like she was having so much fun, plus she had the passion that motivated her to work to elevate our team. I saw success ahead of me again. This time, however, the suit was accompanied by stiletto heels and flip curls. I was drawn to Molly's drive, passion, and humility. I wanted to be like her.

I had a patient who'd had surgery on both eyes and couldn't see my face. I attended to her in recovery, and she said I was just the person she needed to be her nurse. She asked my name, and when I said my first name only, she asked for my last name. When I told her, she smiled and said, "Ah, Dr. Bruce!" She then proceeded to tell me that I wasn't going to be just a nurse for long. I was going to speak and lead people while heading up a successful business that would grow internationally. She said that I might lose a few people along the way, but that everyone who jumped and stayed on board was going to catch that same fire that burned inside me. She spoke of the things I knew but never shared with anyone. The interesting part was that I had just graduated with my master's degree and had just been approved for doctoral admissions.

Shortly afterward, I was injured at work. The injury was severe, causing a neuro deficit in my leg and foot. Most of the time, I couldn't feel my toes. I couldn't walk, bend over, or sit down, let alone work. As a result, my income plummeted from six figures to around the average household income. It seemed to me that I'd failed again, and, this time, I was completely powerless to take action to change my situation. I had no choice but to be still. Initially, I was angry that this had happened to me, until I suddenly realized that I was actually prepared for the situation and that, in fact, it had happened for me.

The injury slowed me down, gave me time to reflect on just how I'd arrived at that point, what my purpose in life was, and how I could turn my situation into a success. Looking back, I saw that I'd gone through just about every circumstance to prepare me for this challenge.

Around this time, I was shown an opportunity involving network marketing. Without a clear plan, I accepted it and figured I had to act this time. I'd done enough self-reflection to realize that the job I'd valued so much didn't value me at all. I decided it was time to get back to doing things that fulfilled my purpose.

Starting my own network marketing business turned out to be the best decision I ever made in my life. I had all the necessary skills, desire, motivation, and fire already in me to make a go of it. And, yes, that patient was correct: Some people, including family members and friends, refused to come along on the ride. But those that did, I'm happy to say, are sharing the fruits of success right alongside me. For me, helping others reach their financial potential, especially during these tough times, continues to be deeply personally rewarding. I often think about that patient: She was right about my business being a success. One day, I hope to give her a big hug and treat her to a nice lunch.

At this point in my long and sometimes challenging journey through life, I've come to realize that no matter what my job was or how many times I failed in the past, all I needed was to see that my success had no boundaries and that, sometimes, we just need to be shown what success actually looks like.

BIOGRAPHY

Tonika Bruce is a registered nurse, speaker, change agent, and serial entrepreneur with over 20 years of experience in building businesses and teams. She is a 6-figure income earner and shares an insatiable desire for helping others find success, purpose, and prosperity. She relishes living a life of a higher purpose and is the founder of multiple non-profit organizations. Tonika strives to amalgamate her love for serving people and expertise in business to help others unlock doors to financial freedom. Tonika found success in multiple niches, including nursing, entrepreneurship, business and basketball coaching, and executive leadership.

Contact Information
Facebook: https://www.facebook.com/tonikabruce11
Instagram: http://instagram.com/tonikabruce
Website: http://tonikabruce.com

CHAPTER 32

DREAMS ARE FOR SUCKERS

By Whitney Tello

New mom. Divorced. Unemployed. I did not plan for it in my life planner. This was not the life I wanted, but this was, in fact, the life I was living. The *unimaginable* was now my *reality*. Fate played a cruel joke on me, and within eighteen months, my entire life changed its course.

Several months after my son was born, my marriage of five years began to fall apart. Soon after, things spiraled rapidly out of control and I was left with the hardest decision of my life—be a single mother or stay in an unhealthy relationship. Even though the force of habit lured me to stay, I knew it wasn't right. I was worth more. If I had stayed in that same situation, I would have settled for much less than I deserved.

I spent sleepless nights, frustrated, why could he not see my love for him? *Why could he not see what he had right in front of his face?* Such thoughts occupied my mind. He had a wife that adored him and a 'brand-new' perfectly healthy baby boy. This was supposed to be *our* time. We spent two of our five years of marriage dealing with the dreaded pains of infertility. Our son was supposed to be our beacon of light, our reward for all our pain and suffering. Little did I know, my suffering through the years of infertility was minuscule when confronted with the devastation of a broken marriage.

Imagine two people in a rowboat with stationary oars, both of them responsible for rowing their oars. But if they do not row in harmony, that boat is not going anywhere anytime soon. Much like that boat, my marriage was moving in circles with no clear destination in sight. After endlessly rowing alone, my arms refused to budge. I filed for divorce. I had a surprise in store for me. Two weeks after my divorce finalized, I was let go from my job—a job in which I was recently promoted and was on track to achieve much more.

I was in the boxing ring of life, 12 rounds in and exhausted. Life was throwing all its best punches at me. I was knocked down but not yet knocked out. I had a choice: do I continue onto the 13th round, or do I give up? I could faintly hear the referee counting to 10 as my inner monologue kicked in.

"Why is this happening to me?"
"What else could go wrong?"
"This isn't fair."
"I didn't sign up for this."
"Why can't I catch a break?"
"What am I going to do?"
"You'll figure it out."
"Can he stop counting already and let me think?"
"*Get up.*"

I got up. Shaken and confused, but I carried myself into the 13th round and beyond. I realized that life takes unexpected turns. The choices of others, both indirectly and directly, affect you. Trauma and loss are intricately woven in the circle of life. At first, I focused on *why*. But those questions led me nowhere, except down a rabbit hole of confusion and dismay. I was asking the wrong questions; I needed to ask *how*.
"How will I get out of this situation?"
"How will I provide for my son as a single mother?"
"How will I show my son that he has a strong and resilient mother?"
"How will I create more time and achieve financial freedom?"
"How will I ensure that my financial future is in my own hands?"
"How do I wish to be remembered?"

"How will I pass on my legacy to my son if I don't start it *now*?"

Although I never desired to be an unemployed, single mother, and the circumstances were wildly out of my control, there was *one* thing that was still under my control—my actions. What I did about it was 100% my responsibility. I got up before the referee got to 10. I put my future back in my own hands. I regained control of my life and put myself in the driver's seat again.

Accepting your reality does not mean understanding your reality; there is a difference. Merely possessing knowledge doesn't produce results. People often talk about how they know what they should be doing, but they aren't doing it. So, I threw in the towel in trying to make sense of my new life. I leaned into accepting rather than understanding, and changes started to happen, slowly but surely. I made a decision that *why* no longer mattered, but *what* I am going to do about it, does.

Education doesn't prepare you for life. Only life can prepare you for life.

Are You a Sucker?

Have you ever been suckered, much like me, at a young age, to buy into the mentality that you should follow your dreams? To think that you should always believe in yourself? Or even believe that you can be anything you want to be in this world? Did you also believe that if we go to school, get into a good college, get good grades, land a good job, get married, and have kids, life would be all fine and dandy? So why is it I was a divorced, single mother, and unemployed even with a degree in business? I checked all the "right" boxes exactly how society taught me, but life still happened.

Once we transition into adults, 'dreaming big' is criticized, dismissed, rejected, and even mocked. "Aim for the stars" fades into the stern noise of "be grateful for what you have." Is it wrong to want more? Be more? Do more? It wasn't wrong for a child, then why so for an adult?

We've all heard the phrase money doesn't buy happiness. That is true. However, we also fail to mention that money does provide the means to create the lifestyle you desire for your own level of happiness. Does gardening bring you happiness? Money enables you to pay for the soil, plants, or gardening tools. Does traveling with your family bring you happiness? How do you pay for the gas, flights, accommodations, food, etc.?

Once I purged myself of self-sabotaging thoughts that I do not deserve more, I went for it at full speed. I have now found a life full of happiness and purpose. My mantra still rings true now as it did at the beginning of the 13th round: I don't want money to be rich, I want money to *enrich*. Yes, you can do both—have money and still enrich the lives of others.

I Will Ask Again, Are You a Sucker Too?

Have you accepted your reality? Are you ready to be in the driver's seat? You create the life you want. You determine your future. It's up to you to bring your vision to life.

If you have a vision, do you see it clear as day? Do you live it and speak it into existence? Good, then you're a sucker too. Welcome to the club! You got that vision, right? Everything in life, including your success, depends on you *protecting your vision*. You are the gatekeeper of your vision. The only person truly stopping you from living your dream life is you.

BIOGRAPHY

Whitney Tello is a self-made entrepreneur who fought her way to the top when life knocked her down. From becoming a first-time mother to a divorcee to an unemployed single mother, Whitney was still determined to leave her mark on this world. Growing up thirty minutes outside of New York City, Whitney was accustomed to dreaming big. With a degree in Business and Spanish, and digital marketing expertise, she jumped two feet in when it came to starting a career in network marketing. Now through years of self-development and self-discovery, Whitney has made it her mission to help others get unstuck in life by sticking to their dreams and transforming them into realities. Some of her many passions include spending quality time with her son, fitness, travel, and never giving up on her lifelong quest to master the art of making the perfect pancake.

Contact Information
Facebook: https://www.facebook.com/13TeenthRound/
Instagram: https://www.instagram.com/whittywits/
Website: https://www.13teenthround.com/regain-control

THE END